HAUNTED
EASTERN PANHANDLE OF WEST VIRGINIA

HAUNTED EASTERN PANHANDLE OF WEST VIRGINIA

JUSTIN A. STEVENS

Published by Haunted America
A division of The History Press
An imprint of Arcadia Publishing
Charleston, SC
www.historypress.com

First published 2025

Manufactured in the United States

ISBN 9781467158299

Library of Congress Control Number: 2025940399

To the good people of the Eastern Panhandle,
both past and present, in the physical and spiritual realms.

CONTENTS

ACKNOWLEDGEMENTS

The road to the finish line of writing this book has been fraught with challenges and setbacks. I frequently found myself haunted by looming deadlines and a MacBook that was determined to frustrate me with its non–user friendly little quirks! The research process was sprinkled with promising leads that turned into dead ends and people who promised to share their story who later ghosted me! All joking aside, this book has been a monumental research passion project that never could've reached completion without the assistance of some key individuals.

Jessie Norris provided tremendously helpful information and very generously provided a wealth of stories from her vast catalog of Middleway lore. Her enthusiasm for the town and its history and legends is contagious. Jamie Bryant graciously provided a highly coveted, next-to-impossible-to-find resource that was the key to some vital information. The people of Shepherdstown deserve special recognition for their willingness to help point me in the right direction for certain stories and locations, as well as for eagerly sharing extremely beneficial information about their beloved town. Angie Knight Manuel helped educate me on Charles Town's haunts. My ghost-loving sidekick Rose Carter always kept an ear out for a good story and enthusiastically accompanied me on legend tripping adventures and field research. Locals in Martinsburg provided an endless supply of paranormal experiences and tales passed down from the old-timers. Attendees on the Martinsburg Ghost Tours over the years have provided verification for many of these stories. Matt Umstead was a great supporter of the tours and helped immensely in gaining access to the Martinsburg Roundhouse, much to the excitement of patrons on the tours. Dana Mitchell gave an abundance of extremely well-researched information on Shepherdstown and its ghostly goings-on. The History Press and more specifically my editors, Kate Jenkins and Laurie Krill, deserve special recognition for taking on this project and getting it off the ground—Laurie especially, for her patience with some of the unexpected delays that occurred. By far the biggest shout-out goes to my loving husband and best friend, Marc Messner, who was a constant source of stability and encouragement, whether we were lost on winding, desolate roads or almost passing out from heat exhaustion while hiking up the side of a mountain to get to the cemetery in Harpers Ferry on a scorching hot summer day!

The many people who contributed to this book, no matter how minor or significant the contribution, are all a piece of the building blocks of this publication.

INTRODUCTION

Do you believe in ghosts? Even the most hardened skeptic must admit there are things that frighten us. And there's no denying that there are signs from the dead. In dark places, we hear their whispers, recall their names and wonder why it is that some cannot rest. Restless spirits roam, they say—but why? Is it to seek vengeance? To find relief from guilt? Or to finish a life cut violently short? Sometimes a ghost can look just as real and solid as you and me. But sometimes, a ghost doesn't always have to be seen to be believed.

My maternal grandmother would often recount a chilling experience that occurred after the death of my great-grandfather. She had a dream in which she saw him enter her bedroom. He stood by the doorway with a melancholy expression frozen on his face, his eyes fixated on her. Startled by his appearance, she asked him what was the matter. He replied, "I cannot rest. I'm disturbed." Perplexed by his troubling reply, she inquired as to why he was not at rest and what disturbed him so. Her father approached and flung himself across the bed and my frightened grandmother.

The next day, a nagging sense that something was askew gnawed incessantly at my grandmother. She rode by the cemetery where her father was interred and noticed activity involving workers at his grave site. She approached the men and demanded an explanation for the overturned earth tainting his place of rest. The workers apologized and went on to tell her that while digging the neighboring grave, they inadvertently dug into her father's plot, disturbing the earth surrounding the coffin. Now the pieces of the puzzle rapidly fell into place, making shattering sense. My grandmother felt that she had experienced a visitation from beyond the grave and that it was a genuine supernatural experience.

My grandmother's recounting of this bizarre tale sounded like an episode straight out of *The Twilight Zone*. Her other tales of the uncanny involving her family and herself helped fuel the imagination of my young, precocious mind. My fascination with things that go bump in the night developed into a lifelong journey. Reading ghost story books and relishing in Halloween's annual celebration of all things ghostly and haunted were vivid primers. Family visits to historic sites such as Gettysburg and Harpers Ferry were highlighted by attending their ghost tours. I still have very vivid memories of the late, great Shirley Dougherty's dramatic and compelling storytelling on the Harpers Ferry ghost tour. Her tour is the oldest ghost tour in the United States. I hung on every word of her incomparable delivery each time I had the pleasure of attending one of her tours.

To satisfy my curiosity and hunger for knowledge of the spirit realm, I eventually joined a paranormal team. Visiting allegedly haunted locations and traipsing through the dark using gadgets that were supposed to detect ghosts became an obsession. I eventually channeled my knowledge of the subject into the Haunted History and Legends Tours of Martinsburg, West Virginia, in my hometown. The tours eventually culminated in the book *Haunted Martinsburg*, also published by The History Press.

Nowadays, you won't find me with an EMF reader or a recorder trying to capture disembodied voices or scouting around an old graveyard. My interest in the subject embraces more of the history and lies in uncovering the facts, if any, behind the legends and the reasons for the hauntings. Finding the connection between past events and present-day paranormal occurrences and the common everyday people, not out seeking these situations, who are suddenly thrust into them is what I find so intriguing. The Eastern Panhandle is just a short distance away from the Washington, D.C. metro area. While it was still part of Virginia, the present-day Eastern Panhandle was mostly part of the colonial lands of Lord Fairfax. The panhandle grew when West Virginia was created. It is populated by many small towns and cities, each with their own claim to fame. Berkeley County contains Martinsburg, hometown of the infamous Civil War Confederate spy Belle Boyd. Bunker Hill is home to the Morgan Cabin, the homestead of the first permanent white settler of West Virginia. Jefferson County contains Harpers Ferry National Historic Park, which was the scene of fiery abolitionist John Brown's raid, an event that was a catalyst for the Civil War. Today, tourists from all over the world flock to this major tourist destination. John Brown's imprisonment, trial and execution transpired in Charles Town. Shepherdstown is the oldest town in the state and was the subject of its own television series on Destination America, *Ghosts of Shepherdstown*. Tourists flood the town annually, for both its ghosts and its vibrant small-town Americana atmosphere. Middleway lays claim to one of the state's most famous and documented ghost stories, the Legend of the Wizard Clip.

Collectively, the towns that compose the Eastern Panhandle weave a rich tapestry of Native American, Revolutionary and Civil War history. Generations of people have lived, loved and died in the many aged homes and buildings contained in the historic districts of these towns. Some suffered and faced hardships, and some left this world prematurely, before they were ready to go on to the next plane of existence.

It is my mission with this book to showcase and, hopefully, preserve the preponderance of ghost stories that litter this region. This book is no way a comprehensive collection; that would be enough for more than one volume, easily. Some of the more famous stories that have been published in print, in numerous ghost story collections and online have been eliminated if there wasn't any new or updated information to add. The lesser-known or forgotten stories take the spotlight here and will, hopefully, be preserved to thrill and entertain future generations. Finding the facts that inspired the stories rather than regurgitating the same old tired, inaccurate information was the driving force of this project from its inception to its completion. Some stories from the *Haunted Martinsburg* book are revisited here with updated narratives and newly discovered facts. Historians, tour guides, paranormal researchers and psychics have all been a part of the research process. Join me now on a haunted literary journey through majestic landmarks, shadowy corridors and moonlit cemeteries as we uncover the ghosts of the Eastern Panhandle and reveal their tragic tales of love, loss and unfinished business.

CHAPTER 1
THE HAUNTED THEATER
MARTINSBURG, BERKELEY COUNTY

In the landscape of Martinsburg's historic district, there's a building that proudly stands on the corner of Martin and Spring Streets. Constructed in 1912, it was not the first theater to operate in the town. There had been the Strand and the Central Opera House. By 1910, those theaters were no longer the showplaces they had once been, and there was a need for a new motion picture house. At about this time, a successful businessman by the name of Harry Thorn and his wife, Mary, had just suffered through a devastating tragedy: the sudden death of their son, Edgar. Harry was burdened by such insurmountable grief that his wife thought he should get involved with a project to occupy his mind and his time. The project he chose was the building of a new community entertainment building.

Thorn commissioned Chappie Kent, a local architect, to prepare plans for the new facility. Kent, in turn, commissioned Reginald Geare, a Washington, D.C. architect known for his expertise in designing theaters. One of the theaters he had designed was the famous Knickerbocker Theater in Washington. The new theater had three main levels. The first floor was the main auditorium, which was used for motion pictures, live performances, conventions and other meetings. During the era of silent films, a live Moller organ supplied the soundtrack. In addition to popular movies of the day, vaudeville and minstrel shows and theatrical productions graced the stage. The second and third floors housed the Roseland Ballroom and Thornwood Hall, which were used for a variety of functions, including cotillions, dance classes, annual balls and much more.

The Apollo Theatre. Martinsburg's most famous ghost, George, resides in this historic theater. *Author's collection.*

The Apollo has always been a part of community life in downtown Martinsburg and continues to be an active venue in the performing arts arena; live performances and shows are staged annually. It has always brought people together in positive ways and has been filled with the creative energies of all who have contributed to its success. And like most historic theaters, the Apollo has developed a reputation over the years for having a few ghostly residents that like to give performances of their own.

One often repeated story concerns a saloon that was once located at the present site of the theater. It is said to have been situated where the present stage sits in the auditorium. It is alleged that the establishment housed a "place of ill repute," otherwise known as a brothel. According to local legend, there was a fire one fateful night that incinerated everyone unfortunate enough to be caught inside the structure. Legend has it that the ladies of the night who perished still return to dance on the Apollo Theatre's stage. Cabaret-style music is heard from the otherwise empty house, and ghost hunters have supposedly captured EVP (electronic voice phenomenon) recordings of flirtatious-sounding prostitutes propositioning potential clients.

Research has revealed that there indeed was a saloon and restaurant located at the site of the Apollo. It was a soft drink saloon operated by Frank Martin and F. Vernon Powell, housed in a building known as Turner Hall, which was owned by Mrs. Matilda Schleusse. According to the December 30, 1911 edition of the *Martinsburg Herald*, a fire of unknown origin erupted in the saloon, completely gutting it and damaging the building. The article mentioned no fatalities or injuries that occurred in the blaze. Whether a brothel operated within Turner Hall cannot be confirmed, but if, as local legend has it, a whole saloon full of people had been engulfed in a raging fire, it certainly would have been reported in the local newspapers. Are phantom prostitutes still trying to ply their trade on the Apollo Theatre's stage? This may or may not be taking place at the historic Martinsburg landmark, but I think it's safe to say any such phantoms are not the victims of a tragic fire in the former Turner Hall.

In 2003, a movie about the Civil War called *Gods and Generals* was filmed in the area. The Apollo was selected as a filming location, and it was made up to look like two different theaters, one of them being the Ford's Theatre in Washington, D.C. The cast and crew were gathered out in the lobby, and a female actor wearing Civil War garb went to use the restroom. Moments later, she came running out screaming, stating there was a man in there. A couple of crew members immediately ran in, only to find the restroom vacant. The director of the theater was standing nearby and heard the commotion. He approached the woman and asked her what the man looked like. She said he had a brown beard and was wearing a red flannel shirt with what appeared to be bib overalls and smoking a cigar. However, he was only visible from the waist up. The director told her the description she gave of the man matched that of the ghost of the Apollo known as George.

George is the resident spirit of this theater and is one of Martinsburg's most famous ghosts. For years, there have been sightings of George. During nighttime rehearsals, actors have reported seeing him walking across the balcony. He's also often spotted standing near the windows of the ballroom or leaning over the second pin rail, observing. Sometimes, during performances, certain things happen that can't be explained, like a rocking chair rocking on its own or the light bars swinging back and forth unprovoked. It's said that if George is pleased with a performance, you can smell the strong aroma of his cigar smoke: this is his way of making his approval known. People are startled when they see George, but he seems to be friendly. He is just protective of the theater and watches over it. Most people who have spent any amount of time at the Apollo have had an experience with George or know someone who has.

I'd like to add that there was a strange coincidence surrounding George's death. According to a popular story that the folks around the theater like to tell, George was a technical director at the theater many years ago. He was up on the catwalk working with the pulleys when he lost his footing and fell to the stage floor below. As is the case with most ghost stories, tragedy led to the haunting, which is why George still hangs around the Apollo in spirit. An in-depth look into the facts of this story revealed no documented proof that any such incident ever took place or that any death has ever happened within the walls of the historic structure. However, something happened that may shed some light on the identity of Martinsburg's ghostly celebrity.

In the December 12, 1913 edition of the *Martinsburg Statesman*, it was reported that two young men, George Leslie "Bud" Creque and William Wright, went down to the Baltimore and Ohio Railroad passenger depot. The newspaper was a little murky regarding the details of what exactly happened next, but having pieced together the story from other articles in other news outlets, it seems that while standing on the front porch of the depot, they had some trouble with another gentleman, leading to an altercation in which William Wright assaulted the other man. B&O Railroad Detective B.L. Prince arrived on the scene, arrested Wright and started escorting him into his private office in the B&O Building. Creque interfered and was warned to leave the premises or he, too, would be arrested. Not heeding the orders, he continued, and the officer pushed him aside and warned him again.

One thing led to another, and the confrontation became violent. George picked up a rock and hurled it at the officer, bashing him in the head with a blow so brutal that it knocked him to the ground. He then began running up Martin Street. The officer staggered to his feet, blood oozing from the top of his head and streaming down his face, and drew a .44 caliber British bulldog revolver from his pocket. He fired the gun at his antagonist, and a bullet struck Creque in his right side, exiting his body through his heart. George continued to try to run but staggered and eventually collapsed at the corner of the Apollo Theatre. George Creque was pronounced dead at only twenty-five years of age. He was the only living son of George Edward and Alice V. Creque. He was employed in a local mill as a weaver and was also a member of the Ryneal Hose Company No. 1.

I'd like to add that there was strange a coincidence surrounding George's death. According to the May 28, 1892 edition of the *Martinsburg Herald*, John W. Poisal, George Creque's brother, was working as a bartender at the saloon in Turner Hall. Four intoxicated men became drunk and disorderly, and John tried to throw them out of the establishment. George showed up and tried to assist and was knocked to the ground. The brawl moved out into the street, and one of the men drew his gun and shot and killed John in almost the same exact spot where George would be shot and killed years later. It appears history repeated itself, and it was a coincidence strange enough that locals were puzzled by the bizarre irony.

Folks around the theater say they don't know how they came up with the name George for the spirit; it's just a name that seemed to fit. Perhaps it's not a coincidence. Maybe at the time of his bodily death, his spirit found the refuge it was seeking in the theater, and this is where he's stayed ever since. Perhaps George Creque is the very famous George of the Apollo Theatre!

CHAPTER 2

GHOSTLY ECHOES OF WAR

MARTINSBURG, BERKELEY COUNTY

The roundhouse was dark and empty when the security guard entered it that night several years ago. An arts and crafts event was being held at the roundhouse, and it would soon be bustling with activity and eager participants who would be moving through the historic structure in a steady stream, visiting the many vendors stationed throughout the sprawling space. "What a perfect opportunity to be able to be alone and experience for myself if the rumored stories of hauntings here are true!" Since the gentlemen was providing security for the event, he was given full access to the facility for the night. He thought about all the history and turmoil that had transpired on the property during the Civil War and the many men who labored endlessly there as he drifted off into a deep sleep. He was a very sound sleeper; you couldn't wake him with a stick of dynamite. At around three o'clock in the morning, he emerged from his slumber and heard what seemed to be voices coming from a group of people. He tried to focus his sleepy eyes in the darkness, and in the faint light from the windows, he saw something that made him come to the realization that he was not alone in the vast, empty space. A group of shadowy figures were walking in a line across the turntable. They were audibly talking to each other and having conversations. He couldn't discern any of what was being said but could clearly hear the murmuring voices. It was as if he was seeing a shadowy glimpse of the past: railroad workers going about their business on a typical busy day at the roundhouse. It was as if he himself did not belong there and was merely a witness to something that he was not a part of. The past and the present collided in that moment of time in the still dark of the night.

In the 1840s, Martinsburg became a major depot along the Baltimore and Ohio Railroad, since it was the largest town between Harpers Ferry and Cumberland. The railroad brought tremendous growth to the economy of the town, as well as employment. The original roundhouse that occupied this site was built in 1849. The pit for the turntable in the current structure is from the original 1849 roundhouse. The building has sixteen bays and could handle sixteen locomotives. It was like a prototype of Jiffy Lube, which we have today for vehicles, only it was for locomotives. It is the only cast-iron framed roundhouse still standing in the world.

Martinsburg was a strategic point during the Civil War because it was a major depot along the B&O Railroad. The railroad traversed the east–west boundaries between the North and the South. Both Martinsburg and the railroad were constantly under attack. The town changed hands at least thirty-seven times during the Civil War—three times in one day!

When the Civil War broke out, in June 1861, Colonel Thomas "Stonewall" Jackson was ordered to destroy the Baltimore and Ohio Railroad tracks and

The current Martinsburg Roundhouse replaced the original structure, which burned down during the Civil War. *Courtesy of the Library of Congress.*

the railroad facility in Martinsburg. Union troops were advancing into the area from Williamsport, Maryland, and they did not want them to have the benefit of a working rail line or machine shops. To keep the troops from advancing easily, the beautiful limestone pillared Colonnade Bridge on East Burke Street, gifted to the town as a monument by the B&O, was blown up. Tracks were torn up, and railroad ties were burned. Along with military destruction, there was also confiscation. Valuable railroad equipment and tools were collected, and some of the railroad cars were loaded with coal and torched. The remaining cars were stripped of as much unnecessary weight as possible and outfitted with metal tires. Chains were hitched to teams of thirty-two to forty horses, which pulled the cars up the steep Martin Street hill onto Queen Street to make the journey.

In 1862, after the Battle of Antietam, Stonewall Jackson was given orders to burn down the entire complex along with the original roundhouse. That is exactly what he did. It was a massive inferno; the smoke billowing up into the sky was visible for miles. The people of Martinsburg watched helplessly and with horror as the heartbeat of the town stopped and the economy crumbled and collapsed into destruction. The Berkeley Hotel was the only building spared because it was not owned by the B&O and was not seen as a threat. The current roundhouse, along with the other buildings, was constructed after the Civil War.

Working conditions within the roundhouse were very dangerous in the old days. All the modern safety measures that we have today were not in place. It was not uncommon for deaths and grisly accidents to occur: limbs being lost, fingers maimed or legs crushed. Railroad employees worked hard and fought furiously to rebuild after the devastation of the Civil War. They labored intensely and were very dedicated to connecting our country. Perhaps some of them are still on the job, and their dedication has lasted beyond the grave. The sounds of hammers tapping and indiscernible conversations between gruff, gravelly-voiced men have been heard.

Another ghostly legend associated with the historic site stems from the harrowing confiscation of the railroad cars during Jackson's notorious raid. As one of the lumbering beasts inched up the East Martin Street Hill, drawn by horses, a young girl and her brother were playing at the bottom of the hill with a group of other children. The horses strained to crest the top of the hill, whipped unmercifully by the men riding them. The chain hooked to the car became dislodged, and the car went crashing back down the hill at high speed. The young girl let out a horrified scream as she saw her brother crushed beneath its weight before she and the other children were obliterated

East Martin Street Hill. Teams of horses pulled confiscated railroad cars up this steep hill during Stonewall Jackson's infamous raid of the Martinsburg train station. *Author's collection.*

in a single heart-shattering instant. It all happened so quickly that they didn't have time to react.

They say that if you happen to be in the vicinity around the middle of August, the anniversary of when this tragedy allegedly occurred, you can hear the sounds of horses snorting, metal cracking and the snap of leather followed by a child's bloodcurdling scream as the horrific event replays itself once again. The spirits of the children are also said to haunt the area. People have reported seeing them playing over in the ruins across the street. The Berkeley Hotel is adjacent to East Martin Street and the alleged site of the accident responsible for the demise of the children. There's a children's museum in the lower part of the depot, and visiting children have reported talking to "other children" who are not visible to anyone else. A former employee once heard a child giggling who was not physically present. One night, when she was closing for the night, she was heading upstairs and heard a voice say, "Good night." Other activity reported within the building includes alarms that mysteriously go on and off of their own accord, disembodied footsteps and sightings of a bearded man wearing a hat and a long black coat on the stairway and upstairs.

The roundhouse complex has been investigated numerous times in recent years by paranormal researchers, and the consensus seems to be that it's a real paranormal hot spot. One investigator was alone in the roundhouse one night and heard footsteps running up behind him. He whirled around to see a white, formless mist confronting him that quickly faded from sight. The same investigator reported what sounded like something running around the outside of the building and banging on all the doors and fleeting black hooded figures darting about in the shadows.

The Artifacts Room once housed lots of memorabilia and items from the railroad's past. It contained a photograph of the original pre–Civil War roundhouse. It's been claimed that the room is very paranormally active at times. Two psychics were physically attacked on separate occasions. Each time, both were doubled over with abdominal pain. There was a paranormal conference held at the roundhouse a few years ago: paranormal researchers and investigators from all over gathered for the conference. A former roundhouse tour guide was in the Artifacts Room talking with a psychic medium. As they were chatting, the medium's countenance began to change, and he began looking about the room. He asked the tour guide, "Can you feel it? Something's happening." He began sweating profusely, and the guide watched in astonishment as three scratches formed across the man's face.

Another night, investigators were there with a film crew. While they were gathered in the office, a rancid, sulfuric smell began to fill the air. One investigator felt a sharp, burning pain go through her back. The investigator in front of her was up against the brick wall and felt a searing pain go through her chest. The other investigators came rushing in, and the investigator who felt the intense burning pain on her back urged the others to lift her shirt. Upon doing so, the investigators witnessed three bloody gashes forming across her back. As all of this was happening, an investigator came running in from outside, exclaiming, "Did you see it?" An investigator dashed out the door and immediately snapped photographs, capturing an image of an inhuman type of creature that was on all fours like some kind of animal. She showed it to the other investigator, who said, "That was what I saw!" She explained that she had seen the entity pass through the exterior brick wall of the office. It's often reported that the putrid smell of sulfur indicates the presence of this spirit.

About two years ago, I conducted a Halloween tour of the historic district of Martinsburg that culminated inside the pitch-black roundhouse. When the group moved into the Artifacts Room, I noticed that all the artifacts and items had been moved out of the room; it seemed it was being used to store metal folding chairs. After the tour, a lady approached me and stated, "You won't have any more problems in that room." She went on to tell me that she has been able to see and communicate with spirits ever since having a near-death experience. She stated that the troublesome spirit had been attached to an item housed in the room. When the item left, the spirit went with it. She said it was the spirit of a very angry worker. The item in question was either responsible for or connected to the death of a coworker, and he was trying to keep people out of the room and away from the object to protect others from meeting the same fate as his friend. He had become consumed with bitterness and hatred because of this unknown tragedy that had taken place. Whether the woman was accurate in her reading and whether the room will remain free of the hostile presence remains to be seen.

The bridge shop has had its share of strange happenings. On the second floor, a light is seen moving past the windows. It's described as looking like an old Coleman lantern being carried by someone in shadow. A former volunteer/tour guide and a friend who was with him saw this one night while closing. When they investigated, they found no natural source for the strange light. This has been occurring for many years. It's thought to be the spirit of a former night watchman or caretaker still making his nightly rounds.

Several years back, there was an incident in which a train was unable to get down to the station. The passengers had to make their way down by foot along the Tuscarora Creek. As they were passing a field behind the roundhouse, they noticed a group of Civil War solders in what appeared to be a Union artillery unit pulling out. The group wondered if there was some type of reenactment taking place—until the soldiers looked directly at them and pointed their rifles. The observers saw the muzzle flashes but could not hear gunfire. The entire ghostly mirage seemed to melt away into thin air. At least three people in the group witnessed this ghostly time warp. Back in the '80s, a similar incident was reported when a train was derailed during a snowstorm and the passengers had to trudge through the snow to the train station.

The bridge shop is said to be haunted by a lantern-toting specter. *Courtesy of the Library of Congress.*

Throughout the Civil War, skirmishes were fought in and around the property. Soldiers from both sides fought hard, and lives ended violently. Both Union and Confederate troops are said to have used that field to set up their artillery, depending on who had control of the town. Perhaps they are still doing that on the spiritual plane, unaware that the war ended long ago.

CHAPTER 3

THE DOG POISONER

MARTINSBURG, BERKELEY COUNTY

If you were to stand on the corner of Spring and East Burke Streets, you would see the street sloping down a steep hill and passing beneath a railroad bridge tunnel at the bottom. On the other side of the bridge, you would see the road ascending a very steep hill that leads into an area of town known as Irish Hill. It gets its namesake from the Irish railroad workers who resided there with their families.

It was late one night long ago. An Irishman was walking alone up this hill, making his way to his home on High Street. Most people had retired to their beds for the night, so there was no one else milling about on the darkened street. There was no sound except for the shuffling of his own footsteps as he trudged up the seemingly endless hill in the thick blackness that had blanketed the empty street. He began to feel a slow, creeping feeling of dread. There was something in the air; it seemed to be charged with an energy of unknown origin. The lone traveler became so uneasy that he found himself looking over his shoulder, only to see the old rattling railroad bridge he had just crossed growing smaller and fainter in the distance.

As he turned back around to face the road ahead, he suddenly found himself confronted by what appeared to be three large black dogs blocking his path. They were the size of calves. Their eyes seemed to glow, penetrating their otherwise jet-black appearance. They snarled and growled, and it seemed to the man that they were about to rip his throat out. The only thing he could think of to do in this terrifying moment was to use his religion for protection. He made the sign of the cross and then ran as fast as his legs

East Burke Street Hill. The Hellhounds of Martinsburg are said to descend this hill on certain dark nights of the year. *Author's collection.*

would carry him the rest of the way up the hill. He didn't dare look behind him to see if the spectral canines were in hot pursuit. He didn't stop until he was safely inside his house, where he jumped into bed and threw the covers over his head.

He was not the first or the last to encounter these terrifying creatures. It is said that on certain dark nights of the year, the black dogs make their way from High Street down the East Burke Street Hill. They enter the railroad bridge tunnel, but they do not come out the other side; they vanish from sight. In recent years, I spoke to a man who lives on High Street. He said that very early one morning, before dawn, when it was still dark out, his wife stepped outside. She came running back into the house screaming bloody murder. He tried to calm her down and urged her to tell him what happened that had frightened her so. She said that when she stepped outside, she saw a type of creature hunched over by the garage. It turned in her direction, and her eyes met with what she described as looking like a werewolf.

Local lore has connected these bizarre happenings with the horrific lynching of an African American man, John Tolliver, back in 1874, who was allegedly buried in a ditch outside of the African American Cemetery that adjoins Green Hill Cemetery at the end of East Burke Street. The ghost dogs, it is said, are supernatural avengers of the horrible crime. This theory is explored in depth in the book *Haunted Martinsburg*. However, further research revealed something else shocking and disturbing that adds another intriguing angle to the haunting of this street and neighborhood.

This town has had its share of the murder and mayhem typical of most small towns. While we haven't had any serial killers in the traditional sense, what we did have was a serial dog killer. From 1908 to 1916, dogs were being poisoned around town. In the June 26, 1908 edition of the *Martinsburg Statesman Democrat*, it was reported that several valuable dogs had been poisoned. One of them was a prized bird dog that belonged to the state's attorney Allen B. Noll, who offered a $100 reward for any information leading to the arrest of the perpetrator. The heinous crimes were being committed using meat laced with strychnine, which was left in people's yards and gardens and in the streets. In the September 18, 1909 edition of the *Martinsburg Herald*, it was reported that at least thirty dogs were killed within a two-week period. An investigation was conducted by Allen B. Noll, and he presented indictment charges to the grand jury against a prominent state senator, claiming he had strong evidence that he was the dog poisoner. However, based on my findings, it seems that the indictment never made it to trial.

In the August 19, 1911 edition of the *Martinsburg Herald*, it was reported that the killer had struck again, this time on Irish Hill. More than half a dozen dogs were found poisoned on High Street. At least four of them were dead. Unfortunately, the despicable individual (or individuals) was never brought to justice for the contemptible murder of many of the townsfolk's beloved dogs.

So should you happen to be walking up East Burke Street at a late hour and feel an uneasiness in the air, hear growls and see glowing eyes in the shadows, beware! You may be the next to have encountered the spirits of some of the slain dogs, who have returned in the form of hounds from hell, still searching with a bloodthirsty vengeance for their killer.

CHAPTER 4

HOUSE OF MYSTERY

MARTINSBURG, BERKELEY COUNTY

Nestled atop a hill just beyond the hustle and bustle of Martinsburg's downtown area is one of the city's most cherished historic landmarks. The General Adam Stephen House is a beautiful stone Colonial home situated in an oasis of lush green lawns, towering trees and meticulous landscaping. It's a beautiful, peaceful setting, with the Tuscarora Creek meandering along the edge of the land. What is serene and picturesque by day becomes palpably creepy at night. The tall trees cast shadows across the lawn, and the house is eerily silhouetted against the sky.

Every December, an event takes place at the house called Colonial Christmas. It's staged by the General Adam Stephen Memorial Association, which has maintained the home since the 1960s, when it restored the home and opened it as an historic museum. Years back, after one of these events, the caretaker, the president of the Adam Stephen Memorial Association and a docent were closing the house. The president was closing the shutters in the dining room when he heard the staircase creak and the sound of someone walking. Out of the corner of his eye, he caught a glimpse of someone in the hall passing by the doorway. He called out to the caretaker, thinking it was him, but was puzzled when the caretaker answered from upstairs.

While this was happening, the docent was standing in the driveway. He looked up and saw a man coming out of the front door and onto the porch. He was clean-shaven with long, curly hair and was wearing a white shirt with a ruffled collar and sleeves. What was most startling about his appearance, however, was that he was missing the bottom half of his legs.

The General Adam Stephen House, home of the founder of Martinsburg, General Adam Stephen. Today the house is a museum, where some believe his spirit still returns. *Author's collection.*

He drifted off the porch and up the exterior stone stairs along the outside of the house. The docent followed the figure as it faded from view while heading through the backyard.

This was not the first appearance of this ghostly gentleman, they later learned. The son of a previous caretaker paid a visit to the house one day, and he recalled an incident in which he and the vice president of the association were sitting in the hall one Sunday morning waiting for guests to arrive. As they were sitting there, a most unexpected visitor came down the staircase. He was white, translucent and wearing some type of uniform. Oblivious to their presence, he headed out the door and turned right as if heading to the basement. Many people have speculated that this may be the spirit of General Adam Stephen.

The man who built the house and founded Martinsburg is as mysterious as his home. When I say mysterious, I mean we know he was a surgeon and about his military accomplishments—he was a colonel during the French and Indian War and a major general during the American Revolution—but very little is known of the man himself or his personal life. He was never married and had one daughter, named Ann. No one even knows what he looked like; no portraits or sketches were ever done of him. It's thought that this might be due to a scandal that occurred during the Revolution.

During the Battle of Germantown, General Stephen was dismissed from his military duties and stripped of all military honors on a charge of drunkenness. General Stephen claimed he was innocent and that he'd become an object of hatred to a higher-ranking officer. The "higher-ranking officer" was none other than George Washington, whom the general felt had betrayed him as part of a conspiracy to push him aside so Washington's friend, the Marquis de Lafayette, could be appointed major general, which occurred three days after Stephen's dismissal. When Stephen returned to Martinsburg, he finished laying out his town and became the first high sheriff of Berkeley County. He also ran a distillery, an armory and a gristmill. Construction of the house was probably completed in the late 1770s or early 1780s, but for reasons unknown, by 1789, Stephen had sold the house and left Martinsburg. He moved to the Stone House at the Van Meter Farm, where it's believed he died in 1791. It's been speculated that perhaps public opinion had soured toward him due to the scandal during the Revolution, which led to his departure from his town—but again, no one can be sure of anything, and Stephen remains Martinsburg's man of mystery. It's interesting to note that the ghostly colonial gentleman has been seen heading toward the back of the property, where an embankment leads directly to the site of the flour mill Stephen once operated. This is probably a path he took many times when he resided in the home. The fact that he's missing the bottom half of his legs may be because the terrain has changed and built up over the centuries and he's simply reacting to the environment as it was during that time.

The earliest known documented ghostly activity in the house took place when the Showers family resided there in the early 1900s. The granddaughters would stay with the family during the school week. In the evenings, they would sit in the dining room and do their homework. Every night, they would hear heavy footsteps descending the staircase that would walk down the silent front hall and stop right outside the closed dining room door. Curious to see who was on the other side of the door, they'd open it, only to find no one was there. It's interesting to know that an incident that was documented more than one hundred years ago continues to be reported today. Those disembodied footsteps have been heard time and again, usually when people are alone in the house. Some have described them as sounding like shoes with heels clicking on the wooden floors. During colonial times, men wore buckled shoes with heels.

Could it be that General Adam Stephen still returns to his town, which may have turned against him in life? He suffered a damaging and devastating indignity during the Revolution. Even if he was innocent of the charges against him, his reputation will forever be tarnished throughout history, and his many other accomplishments have lost their merit or been overshadowed by it. If he returns to his former home, maybe he wants to set the record straight and wants the truth to be known. It may be that he still roams the halls of his mansion, haunted by personal disappointments or injustice. Perhaps he doesn't want to be known as Martinsburg's faceless founder.

Many other inexplicable happenings take place in this historic eighteenth-century mansion and on the property. There is a room set up at the back of the house as a doctor's office or surgery room. Adam Stephen received a degree in surgery from the University of Edinburgh before he came to America in 1748 and practiced as a surgeon in Fredericksburg, Virginia. He continued his medical practice when he moved to Berkeley County.

Several years ago, an electrician was doing work at the house in this room. Just outside this room is the back door leading to where a porch was once located. It's a steep drop to the ground. The worker brought a small ladder, which he propped up outside the door so he could easily navigate in and out of the house. The caretaker and another docent were doing work in the backyard. They were quite startled when they looked up from their work to see the contractor make a flying leap out of the back door and frantically run across the backyard, scared out of his mind. He claimed that while he was working in the room, an unseen presence grabbed him by the back of the neck. He was in such a hurry to get out of the house that he didn't even take the time to climb down the mini ladder. He refused to go back into the office to finish the job and wouldn't even go inside to retrieve his tools. A new contractor was sent to complete the work.

Back in the 1920s, a group of train robbers held up a train nearby. A chase ensued, with the police in hot pursuit. The bandits were seen escaping into this house. The police did a thorough search of the property, but the men were nowhere to be seen. The police returned a few more times but still left empty-handed. It was as if the men had somehow mysteriously vanished. The mystery was finally solved when one last search of the house finally resulted in the capture of the men, who said they had escaped through a secret passage into an underground tunnel. A closet by the fireplace in the kitchen concealed a hidden entrance, now sealed off by a wall.

The underground tunnel system that connected several locations in this neighborhood has led to much speculation and ongoing excavation efforts.

The original purpose of the tunnels remains unknown, although many of the tunnels probably made use of the natural caverns underneath the length of the ridge on the eastern edge of Martinsburg. It's believed that the enigmatic tunnels were primarily used as a means of escape, particularly from Indian attacks or the British during the Revolution. Prior to the construction of the stone mansion, General Adam Stephen had previously built a log cabin on the property directly over the cave that accessed the tunnels. Settling on this spot was probably a strategic move on his part.

Back in the 1930s, the owner of the house decided to replace the kitchen floor due to fire damage. When he pulled up the old floorboards, he made a most unexpected discovery. Two human skeletons had been hidden beneath the planks. As with so many things about the house's past, we can only speculate about what happened to the flesh-and-blood humans the skeletons belonged to. Did a homicide or some dastardly deed transpire within these walls long ago? Could restless spirits from an unknown murder still be roaming the halls? The truth will probably forever remain a mystery.

The attic of the house was likely used as slave quarters or for extra storage. Strange noises are heard coming from up there, including the sounds of people walking around. In the 1970s, a docent was standing in the hallway when she noticed a woman wearing a long dress floating down the attic staircase, fading from view in the hallway. During the Colonial Christmas event, docents place their jackets on the attic staircase. A docent once ventured up there to retrieve her coat and had a terrifying encounter with a shadow figure that came down the attic steps, engulfing the already darkened space in total blackness. As it passed right through her, the temperature plunged into what felt like an arctic blast of freezing air that penetrated her very soul. In a panic, she scampered down the steps to the first floor and informed the rest of the docents that she was leaving—whether she had her coat or not. The brave males in the group retrieved it for her. Females have reported being touched and having their hair pulled up there, as well as seeing moving shadowy forms. Some refuse to enter the attic and are overcome with feelings of dread.

A local medium visited the house once and said she saw a group of Union soldiers occupying the attic room. She said they were not wanted in the house, and there was a young woman who was bringing food and water to them. A small window to the right of the room held great importance to them. The window overlooks the railroad, which, as we've discussed, was a major source of contention during the Civil War. She said these soldiers were not aware of the living in their presence, but there was one soldier, who stayed in the back corner of the room, who was quite interactive. She felt this spirit had less-than-wholesome intentions and a rather perverse inclination toward women. She said his name was Tyler; she wasn't sure if that was his first or last name. Anytime a female is touched or feels threatened in this space, this spirit is responsible. Perhaps when the house was used as both a hospital and prison, soldiers were held captive in the attic and perished or were executed and still haven't left their earthly imprisonment.

The train tracks that stretch across the back of the Adam Stephen House are the setting for many manifestations and spectral sightings. Twilight had blanketed the property as the caretaker stepped out onto the porch of the Triple Brick Museum next to the house in the cool evening air. All seemed peaceful and serene until his attention was drawn to a strange anomaly. A green, glowing sphere of light was hovering over the train tracks. As a train began approaching, he watched in awe as it moved away from the tracks and floated down the steps along the side of the house and out into the driveway. Once the train had passed, the green phantasm moved up the driveway and over the tracks, disappearing into the trees.

It was the night of May 16, 1905. The Pittsburgh Express pulled into the Martinsburg Train Station. The engineer rushed into the depot, visibly shaken. He reported that he thought he had struck a man on the train tracks. It was eleven o'clock at night and very dark, so he couldn't be certain. A search was made, and the engineer's fears became a reality. The body of a young man was discovered. He had been horribly mangled, his legs severed and his head terribly smashed in. The remains were those of a twenty-two-year-old man by the name of Michael Casey. Walking to his home on High Street, he was crossing the tracks behind the Adam Stephen House when he was struck and killed by the Pittsburgh Express. He was unmarried and left behind his grief-stricken parents and several siblings. In an eerie twist of fate, almost exactly seven years later, in 1912, his brother, Bernard Casey, also twenty-two years old, was found drowned in Bullfrog Spring less than one hundred yards from where Michael met his tragic fate.

During the Depression years, the hill on which the General Adam Stephen House is situated was known as Cinder Hill. As the trains rattled down the tracks behind the house, they would come around a sharp bend, and pieces of coal would fall off. The poor people would come there to gather up the coal to heat their homes during the winter months. One night, a young mother was out on the tracks gathering the coal and heard the whistle of a train approaching. She quickly stepped off one track and onto the other but failed to notice that a train was rapidly approaching from the opposite direction. She stepped right into its path, and in a most cruel twist of fate, she was struck head-on in the same area where Michael had been killed in the same fashion.

Others have reported seeing the strange green sphere in the same area. Some have described it as a hideous green crawling mist that seems to manifest over the tracks in that area. It's a well-known theory that spirits are usually earthbound due to tragedy or a sudden, violent death. Perhaps the young woman's spirit or that of Michael Casey remains trapped on the earthly plane due to their sad, shocking ends on the tracks.

There are also reports of another specter known as the Priest. In the late night or early morning hours, a strange man wearing religious garb and swinging a lantern has been seen roaming the tracks and the hill behind the Adam Stephen House. According to oral tradition in town, Martinsburg was a station on the Underground Railroad for slaves escaping from the South into the Northern states. The underground tunnel system provided the perfect hiding place and escape route. Free African Americans, Good Samaritans and clergymen were often those who sheltered and assisted slaves at the designated stations. There's a theory that perhaps the phantom priest was aiding the slaves by leading them into the tunnel entrance in the house's cellar. In Martinsburg, there were a lot of Confederate sympathizers, and many of the wealthy property owners owned slaves. Perhaps the priest was caught in the act and shot and killed on the property and his spirit remains, still signaling the runaway slaves with the swing of his lantern.

Speaking of the cellar, according to a family who lived in the house in the 1950s, there were once slave shackles in one of the ancient walls. At night, the family would be awakened by the unnerving sound of the chains clanking and rattling against the stone wall. After repeatedly being disturbed by the possessed chains, the father permanently removed them from the cellar.

A group of children was down there on one occasion on a tour, and an unexpected visitor showed up in a photograph. The outline of a headless man holding a lantern was standing in front of the cave entrance.

Across from the Adam Stephen House is the Triple Brick Museum. The building was constructed in 1875 by Philip Showers when the Showers family lived on the property. It was originally divided up into three apartments for railroad workers and their families. Today it houses antiques, memorabilia and historical items from Martinsburg's past.

The caretaker has lived on the property for many years and resides in an apartment within the building. When he first moved in, he would return home and find that a picture of his sister that was on display had been turned around and was facing the wall. After this happened repeatedly, he decided to put the picture away because it seemed that someone or something had a bit of an issue with it.

On a separate occasion, some friends from England came to visit. They headed out for a little excursion and placed a traveling bag on a chair in the living room before locking up. When they returned from their trip, they discovered that the bag had been moved from the chair and was sitting in the middle of the room with the straps standing straight up. The apartment was securely locked, and no one had a key.

One night, the caretaker awoke in the middle of the night and saw an unwanted visitor darkening the bedroom door. An elderly man was peering in, staring straight at him. The poor caretaker pulled the covers over his head to block the apparition from his sight, hiding himself from the dead man's prying eyes. Another person who used to live there would wake up in the same bedroom and see not just the elderly man but also an elderly woman standing in the room, they would watch intently as fear mounted in the former resident from the uncomfortable stares of the intruders. Footsteps are heard walking up and down the stairs, and the scent of a woman's perfume drifts through the room, instantly drawing attention to the sudden sweet scent. A family who lived in an apartment on the other side of the building many years ago claimed that during the night, they would hear a baby's cries coming from within the otherwise quiet, empty building.

According to the son of a previous caretaker, there was a wall in the building that had a bloodstain on it. He painted over it only to have it reappear. After a few more attempts, the association's president had him completely tear out the wall. This raises many questions and leads one to wonder what happened that resulted in blood being splattered on the wall, permanently staining it. Was it a haunting reminder of a bludgeoning that took place long ago? Was there a violent crime committed against someone that remains unknown, and the ghosts of the past are trying to tell us what happened? Many people lived and died on the property, and their hopes and dreams, sorrows and losses played out within these walls. The Adam Stephen House property seems to hold its secrets close. Perhaps it is haunted by memories of the past and those who once called it home and whose lives were touched by it in some way. The many paranormal encounters by scores of people through the years prove that once you've visited a property and appreciated its beauty and uniquely rich history, you want to return, even in spirit!

CHAPTER 5
A SHOT RANG OUT
MARTINSBURG, BERKELEY COUNTY

Through the years, people working in City Hall on Main Street in downtown Martinsburg have reportedly, on occasion, heard something very strange in front of the building: horses thundering down the street and then the sound of a single gunshot, followed by the sound of a lone horse clopping away. They walk outside only to find nothing that could correlate to what they've heard. There may be an explanation for these very odd sounds.

At the time of the Civil War, there was another building located where City Hall is. It was the Valley House Hotel, and there was a restaurant in the lower part of it. Near the end of the Civil War, a Union officer, Lieutenant Ed Gruberman of the First New York Lincoln Cavalry, was eating his lunch when a Union sympathizer informed him that the Confederate cavalry was riding into town. He finished his lunch, got up, went outside the building and waited. He watched as the Confederates came into view, riding down Queen Street. As they approached, he casually drew his pistol, aimed and shot the lead officer off his horse. The rest of the soldiers brought their horses to an abrupt halt. The Union officer nonchalantly strolled over, mounted his horse and rode away as the now leaderless Confederate soldiers looked on in disbelief. They were so stunned by the brash and bold behavior of the Yankee that they didn't even draw their guns or make any attempt to retaliate.

There is a theory that there is a type of haunting known as an imprint, a kind of recording of a traumatic or emotional event that replays itself over and over like a broken record and doesn't involve an intelligent spirit that can interact with the living. If there is any truth to this theory, perhaps that is why this audible haunting continues to startle people who happen to be in the right place at the right time to hear it.

CHAPTER 6

THE NOCTURNAL VISITOR

MARTINSBURG, BERKELEY COUNTY

The young boy was sound asleep in his bedroom upstairs in the stately Crawford-Silver house that proudly occupies the corner of Queen and South Streets in the affluent Tuxedo Row neighborhood of Martinsburg. Perhaps he sensed he was not alone in the darkened room, because for whatever reason, he awoke from his peaceful slumber. His sleepy eyes scanned the room, searching for the source of the uncomfortable feeling of unease that had gripped him. His eyes met with the figure of a man standing at the back of the room. He stood motionless, and the startled boy could feel the penetrating gaze of the intruder's eyes. As the man emerged from the shadows, the boy could see that he was wearing a blue uniform like that of a Union soldier during the Civil War. His heart raced as the figure began approaching his bedside. As he came into sharper focus with each step, the boy noticed that there appeared to be a strange glow illuminating the outline of the soldier. His blood turned ice cold as the soldier stood directly over him, paralyzing him with fear with his intense scrutiny. In a fight-or-flight moment, the terrified boy jumped out of his bed and dashed across the hall to the safety of his parents' bedroom. He hopped onto their bed and shook them frantically to awaken them from their nocturnal sojourn. Groggily, they asked their son what was wrong, trying to abstain from showing their irritation at having been awoken so suddenly. The boy frantically told them about the spectral visitor in his bedroom. His parents tried to console him by telling him he had only been

The Gray Silver House. The Boyd family home, where Belle Boyd famously shot a Confederate soldier, was originally located on this property. *Author's collection.*

dreaming and there was no such person in his room, chalking it up to the "monster under the bed" fear that most small children have at that age. Much to his dismay, the boy was again gripped with terror as he saw the imposing soldier entering his parents' bedroom and approaching their bedside. He frantically pleaded with his parents, telling them that the man was in their bedroom and was approaching. They drowsily looked in the direction of the boy's pointing finger but saw nothing, and unconvinced that there was anything of concern in their bedchamber, they rolled over and retired from the reality of their panicking child. Once again, the soldier stood beside the bed with the same piercing gaze as he loomed over the poor defenseless boy. The morning rays of the sun began to shine through the windows with the break of dawn, and much to the boy's relief and amazement, the soldier began to fade from view.

The Crawford-Silver house was built circa 1895 by W.H. Crawford, who was the owner of the Crawford Woolen Mills. He resided there until he built another house on this street circa 1905. It then became the home of Gray Silver, who was a West Virginia state senator. Both his son and his grandson were judges in Martinsburg. At the time of the Civil War, there was another

Belle Boyd, the infamous Confederate spy who began her espionage activities in Martinsburg. *Courtesy of the Library of Congress.*

house located on this property. It was the home of Benjamin Reed Boyd and his family. They were staunch supporters of the Confederacy.

It was July 4, 1861, and Benjamin was away serving in the Confederate army. The town was occupied by Union troops under the command of General Patterson who were having a noisy Independence Day celebration. The soldiers ransacked a local distillery and eagerly consumed the alcohol. A local Unionist informer told the troops that there was a Confederate flag hanging in one of the bedrooms of the Boyd house. The soldiers rampaged through the house in search of the flag, breaking furniture, smashing family heirlooms and threatening Ben Boyd's horrified wife and family with all manner of violence. When the men failed to find the flag, they proposed raising a Union flag over the Rebel household. Mrs. Boyd refused. She stood beside her seventeen-year-old daughter, Belle, and said, "Men, every member of my household will die before that flag shall be raised over us." The soldiers erupted in anger at the provocative statement and damned the arrogant Rebel women. Belle, furious over the entire incident and outraged at the treatment of her mother, pulled a pistol from the folds of her skirt and shot and killed one of the men. While the Union provost marshal did not press charges against Belle because of the damage to the Boyd home and the drunken condition of the soldiers, the incident transformed her into a fiery enemy.

Belle Boyd immediately began to collect information about the Union army's troop strength, disposition and plans by charming information from Union officers. She always got the information swiftly to nearby Confederate leaders. Among them were J.E.B Stuart during the Union invasion of the lower Shenandoah Valley in 1861 and Stonewall Jackson during his Shenandoah Valley campaign. Belle was arrested on orders from the War Department in Washington, D.C., and imprisoned for her activities. She escaped to England in 1863 because she was, by that time, subject to the death penalty for treason. While there were innumerable spies for both sides who plied their secret trade in the lower Shenandoah Valley during the Civil War, Belle Boyd is said to have been the most romantic and cunning of them all.

Other strange things have been reported at the home. Workers doing renovations a few years back would hear footsteps upstairs while working down in the basement, and a locked door would mysteriously unlock itself and open. Even though the Boyd family home is long gone, perhaps the slain soldier remains behind, unaware of his death.

CHAPTER 7

JAIL AND HOSPITAL HAUNTS

MARTINSBURG, BERKELEY COUNTY

The old stone building has stood on the corner of King and Spring Streets since 1796, when it was built as the Berkeley County Jail. It replaced the original jail, built in 1774, that was housed in the town square. During its original incarnation as a jail, the back of the building, enclosed by a thick, high stone wall, served as a jail yard for the prisoners. It's said that in the yard, many necks were "stretched" in the pillory, a wooden device with holes for the head and hands to be thrust through, locking the victim in place for public humiliation. An alley beside the building housed a public whipping post. When a prisoner was convicted of a misdemeanor, they were given a choice: they could either serve time in the jail or be flogged at the whipping post. It is said that often, flogging was the punishment of choice due to poor conditions in the jail. The only two documented lynchings in the history of Berkeley County involved African American men who were forcibly removed from the jail by angry lynch mobs and subsequently hanged. During the Civil War, both Union and Confederate soldiers stored ammunition in the jail and used the facility as a prison and a field hospital. It's been alleged that the soldiers would amuse themselves with the prisoners by placing them on a blanket and having a wager to see how high they could toss them into the air without dropping them.

In 1894, the jail was becoming overcrowded, and it was decided that a bigger, more modern building was needed. A new jail was constructed on South Raleigh Street. In that same year, this building was put up for sale. It was purchased and converted into a hospital by a Catholic charity order of

Kings Daughters Hospital. The limestone structure was the second Berkeley County jail before it was a hospital. *Author's collection.*

nuns known as the Kings Daughters who had been wanting to establish a hospital in Martinsburg. Up until that time, most of the care of the sick was done at home by family members or at the town poorhouse. In 1896, the building reopened its doors as the Kings Daughters Hospital, Martinsburg's very first hospital. It served in that capacity for the next fifty-eight years until a larger, more modernized hospital was built next to it in 1954 under the management of the Sisters of the Holy Ghost. The hospital eventually merged with the Martinsburg City Hospital and officially closed in 1981. The building is now an assisted living facility under the name of Kings Daughters Court. The original stone structure has been repurposed many times over the years and has been converted into apartments.

The old jail/hospital has a very long and varied history involving many deaths and a lot of human suffering. Many lives began and ended within its walls. Given its grim past, it has developed a reputation as one of the most haunted buildings in all Martinsburg.

One of the most popular tales told about the building involves an African American nurse who supposedly fell in love with her white male patient. They knew that prejudiced minds of the period would never accept their relationship, so it ended, much to the detriment of the nurse's mental health. It is said that the anguished woman went to the top center window of the hospital and threw herself out, plunging to her death on the pavement below. There is no official record of any such incident ever happening. However, I did uncover an interesting snippet in the August 21, 1916 edition of the *Martinsburg Evening Journal*, headlined "She Didn't Jump." It stated that an African American girl who was a patient at the hospital had jumped out of a window while not in her right mind. Hospital administration denied the incident. This brief announcement in the journal bears a remarkable resemblance to the legend.

To add another layer to the enigma, I spoke with a former tenant of one of the apartments who had an interesting bit of information to share. She told me that one day, she was outside smoking a cigarette when she noticed a group of elderly nuns curiously walking about the premises. She struck up a conversation with them and was informed that they had once worked at the hospital many years ago and were revisiting Martinsburg and the site of their former employment. The eldest nun began recounting some memories of the old hospital and stated that there was a tragedy that had occurred. A sick infant was admitted to the hospital who couldn't be saved by the nuns. The child perished, and its grief-stricken mother ended her life by jumping from the top center window, just like the sorrowful nun from the legend. If this incident really took place, was the mother the African American girl who didn't jump, according to the *Evening Journal*? Perhaps the hospital staff feared scandal and unfavorable publicity about someone taking their own life while under their care. We'll never know for sure, but as is the case with most legends, there does seem to be a kernel of truth embedded within the folklore.

Many claim that a scream can be heard coming from the notorious window that travels down the building and ends in a thud, as if a body struck the pavement. One gentlemen told me that a woman shared a personal encounter with him. The lady said she was driving down the street when she happened to look in the direction of the building and saw a reddish figure jumping from the top window. Startled by what she saw, she slammed on her brakes, causing the driver behind her to slam on her brakes to avoid a collision. Both drivers had witnessed the suicidal person's plunge. They quickly approached the building, fully expecting to see either a dead body or at least a very seriously injured person lying on the pavement. To their astonishment, there was absolutely nothing to indicate that what their eyes had seen had happened.

Another local stated that one hot, humid July night, he was taking a late-night stroll. When he passed the front façade of the darkened building, the air became so frigidly cold that he could see his breath in front of him. Once he had passed the old stone building, the sweltering heat of the night returned. A paranormal investigator from Gettysburg who had heard this story took photographs one night to try to capture any ghostly anomalies that might appear. A photograph of the alleged suicide window revealed a glowing human form standing on the ledge as if prepared to step off and fall to the awaiting concrete sidewalk below.

One of the building's many incarnations was a residential home for the mentally impaired, operated by East Ridge Health Systems. While the building was ancient and a bit creepy, it seemed as though it should be able to adequately meet the needs of the individuals who were being housed within its walls. Its history as a hospital whose mission was meeting the needs of the sick and providing healthcare to all, regardless of their means or their ability to pay, was perfectly aligned with the group home's mission.

The supervisor of the facility had two daughters who worked with her there, caring for handicapped individuals. One night, one of the daughters awoke in her bed in one of the group home's rooms and noticed movement in the doorway out of the corner of her eye. Through the open door, she saw the slender shape of a woman wearing a long dress with long, silky blond hair cascading down her back. The woman was walking slowly down the hall, headed in the direction of the door that led to the stairwell. She anxiously observed the ethereal woman, expecting her to open the door and exit, but the woman was extinguished from sight before her hand reached the doorknob. When she told her sister about her experience of witnessing the strange female, she was more than a little surprised to learn that her sister had also seen the same exact woman on occasion. However, her experience varied a bit from her sister's: the wraithlike woman had completed the task of turning the doorknob and opened the door, exiting onto the staircase.

This was not the only strange thing the sisters would encounter during their tenure in the historic structure. On another night, one of the sisters awoke in the same room and was jolted by a vision of four nuns, clad in black robes, gathered around her bed staring down at her, as if she was a patient they were observing. Yet another encounter transpired that was even more chilling than the previous ones when a baby monitor was placed in a room with one of the patients. While the sisters were in another area of the building, their blood ran cold and their scalps prickled when they heard a female voice shrieking over the monitor, "Help me! Help me!" It was not the voice of the patient housed in that room.

One of the darkest chapters in Martinsburg's history was the Spanish influenza epidemic of 1918. It swept across the country, leaving destruction in its wake. The worst effects in Berkeley County came during October and November. More than five hundred people died in Berkeley County. One hundred of those people died in one day. State's Attorney Allen B. Noll was hired to handle the situation in Berkeley County. The Sheriff's Department sent people to check on sick families. In several instances, they found entire families dead from the flu. Churches canceled services, public meetings were closed, businesses operated on limited hours and all theaters in the town were shut down. City Hospital and Kings Daughters Hospital were full and manned by a reduced staff. Many caregivers themselves fell ill and died from the flu. Very few funerals were held during this time because the family members of the deceased were often too ill themselves to attend their loved ones' funerals. Graves could not be dug quickly enough. The town ran out of medicine and caskets, and the gravediggers of the cemeteries couldn't keep up with the ever-mounting accumulation of corpses. Temporary morgues and hospitals were put into place to try to manage the insurmountable devastation. Sadly, all the approximately five hundred people who perished ended up in unmarked graves in Green Hill Cemetery.

Occupants of the apartments in the old building have reported shadowy figures, moving objects, appliances turning on of their own accord, mysterious puddles of water and more, plaguing some of the residents who have resided within. Perhaps these strange things that happen are not just seemingly random events but are echoes of a story from over a century ago. Only 203 of the victims were ever officially recorded; the rest lie forgotten and alone in the boneyard, their names lost to the passage of time. Perhaps they reach out to the living, desperate for recognition, wanting their tragic stories to be known.

CHAPTER 8

GRAVE TALES

MARTINSBURG, BERKELEY COUNTY

The night sky cast eerie shadows across the tombstones that littered the landscape of the Old Norbourne Cemetery as the woman and her boyfriend entered its gates on that long-ago night in the 1980s. They had heard many rumors about the strange things that were said to happen there in the dead of night and were curious to see if they would experience anything for themselves. The old former churchyard was the oldest cemetery in Martinsburg, having been given to Trinity Episcopal Church by Adam Stephen in 1772. The original English Church, as it was known, was long gone, having moved to its present location on King Street in the 1830s. The cemetery now sat surrounded by a weatherworn stone wall containing the many occupants buried within its hallowed grounds. The couple stepped cautiously on the soft, uneven earth, navigating the labyrinth of ornately designed Victorian monuments, crosses and obelisks in the silent, twilight atmosphere.

They decided to split up: the woman's companion went to one area of the cemetery, and she went to the other, carefully observing her surroundings for anything out of the ordinary in the environment. Her eyes were drawn to one particular statue, the only life-size statue in the entire burial ground. It was a marvelously crafted statue of an angel dripping with Victorian opulence. It was beautiful and yet a little creepy, she thought, as it commanded her attention. As she admired the statue, she noticed that there seemed to be a faint glow or a haze materializing around it. As she continued to study this strange anomaly, she realized that the glow was becoming brighter and was illuminating the entire angel sculpture, bathing it in a bright, brilliant light. To her astonishment, a glowing white figure began to emerge from the statue and became mobile, wandering among the weathered tombstones as it navigated through its earthly surroundings. The woman wondered if she could be seeing this phenomenon unfolding right before her very eyes or if she was just having some type of incredible hallucination brought about by the adrenaline rush of the unnerving setting and experience. Once the luminescent figure reached the other end of the cemetery, it turned completely black, devoid of all light, before it vanished from sight.

Determined to prove to herself that what she saw was not some type of hallucination or mirage, she decided to return to the cemetery a week later. This time, she brought people with her, so if the same ghostly scenario replayed itself again, she would have witnesses. As the group crossed the threshold of the entrance gate, they were stopped dead in their tracks by a terrible, guttural-sounding growl that didn't sound like any animal of this earth. Refrigerated by fear, everyone in the group turned and quickly exited the cemetery, removing themselves from the area as fast as they possibly could.

The seemingly bewitched statue marks the grave of Elise Parks, the daughter of Alexander Parks, arguably one of the most successful businessmen in Martinsburg. He operated a distillery, a mill and the National Fruit Company. Elise's family lived in what is now the McFarland House on Queen Street. Elise had a lingering illness; she had been an invalid for several years, and her parents had done everything in their power for her comfort. She suffered greatly during her illness, and death came as a relief when she very suddenly passed away just a few months away from her twenty-fifth birthday. Her grieving father had this statue placed over her grave as a memorial to her. The graveyard was very badly vandalized many years ago, and the statue was toppled over. It was missing its head and arm until a few years ago, when the cemetery underwent a massive restoration. The statue was fully restored and returned to its former glory.

Locals who played there as children recall being very afraid of this statue for some unknown reason. Many have reported a very heavy feeling surrounding it. A man who sometimes walks his dog in there said that the dog refuses to go anywhere near the angelic statue. Perhaps it's psychically charged with some type of spiritual energy. After being an invalid for much of her young life, perhaps, in spirit, Elise returns from her eternal burial place, walking the graveyard with the freedom to do what she, unfairly, was robbed of in life.

The only life-sized statue in Norbourne Cemetery marks the grave of Elise Parks. For years, the statue lay toppled over, missing its head and arm, before it was fully restored. *Author's collection.*

However, she's not the only restless spirit that roams Old Norbourne Cemetery.

A group of intrepid ghost hunters stalked the grounds of the historic site one night in the early 1990s. Like the woman and her boyfriend, they, too, were seeking evidence of the supernatural. A young woman, along with her mother and a friend, branched off from the rest of the group and headed to the far left corner of the cemetery—said to be the most haunted area, where locals warned visitors never to venture. They had heard all the rumors and whispers about the sprawling, gnarly old tree, referred to as the hanging tree, that once loomed over the edge of the property, surrounded by a grove of majestic trees lining the allegedly cursed area. Local legend states that a fiendish man was hanged from one of the sturdy branches of the old tree for committing a brutal act of sexual assault and the murder of a poor, innocent woman. They say that his evil soul still lurks in the impenetrable darkness that blankets the area in the dead of night.

The three woman approached the area cautiously, even as a nagging, ominous feeling of dread began to envelop them. They positioned their cameras, prepared to take photographs of the black mass of shadows that seemed to swallow them. Many people had spoken of the intense fear and nauseating heaviness that would cause some to become physically ill to the point of vomiting until they vacated the negative energy field. Despite the palpable change in the atmosphere and the damp cold that began to wash over them like a cold shower, they were determined to accomplish what they'd set out to do. They began snapping pictures in quick succession. Lit by one of the flashes from the cameras, a dark figure suddenly appeared in front of the women. With his imposing presence and large build, he towered over them. The man, wearing a black cape and a top hat, was missing a face. Just as quickly as he appeared, he turned and ran past the trees, escaping into the deep shadows that engulfed them. One of the eyewitnesses recalled that she had never been so afraid in her entire life as she was in that moment.

A thorough search of the historical archives has revealed nothing to substantiate that a hanging ever took place on this property, but there seems to be some type of malevolent spirit that continues to make its presence known here in sometimes terrifying ways. People claim to have been violently pushed to the ground by unseen hands or chased by an invisible pursuer. The smell of freshly turned-over earth is said to herald the presence of this particular spirit, or a pair of bright red eyes pierces the shadows.

Another group that was investigating the cemetery had a participant who got more than she bargained for. She, too, braved the dreaded area. When

Old Norbourne Cemetery. The left back area is said to have once been the site of an old hanging tree. It is the most paranormally active spot in the historic cemetery. *Author's collection.*

she heard footsteps approaching her, fear took over, and she immediately removed herself and began heading out of the cemetery. The faster she walked, the faster the footsteps dogged her heels. When she reached the gate, an unseen hand grabbed the necklace she was wearing. Instinctively, she clutched the charm that adorned it as the chain was ripped from her neck. She returned the next day in the safety of daylight to search for the necklace only to find it draped over a tombstone.

This fearful apparition seems to be one of the most active resident spirits of this historic burial ground. Visitors report feeling a palpable sense of dread or being overtaken by sudden feelings of rage or hatred when near this corner of the cemetery. A particularly talented psychic medium with a keen sense visited this cemetery with me to solve the mystery of this haunting. Without any prior knowledge of the story of the hanging, she immediately was drawn to the ominous grove of trees and described crossing into a river of evil, visually represented by a black, vaporous mist that flowed down from the trees to the ground, spilling out into the surrounding area. She saw the mist rise and form into the figure of a man wearing what she described as a Jack the Ripper–type costume. She described a hanging that took place from an old tree long gone. She claimed the man had raped and murdered a woman and was hanged for his heinous crime. However, she thought, there was more than meets the eye going on here. She felt that the man was only a part of the collective negative energy that embodied this entity and that he was a disguise for a darker manifestation that had been bound to this location for a very long time. She described a type of conscious dark thought form that had taken on a life of its own, the creation of layers of negative energy and events that had been deposited on the land on which the cemetery is situated. If this is true, what transpired here that was so dark and of such a low vibration in the spiritual realm that created this entity?

In the February 14, 1891 edition of the *Martinsburg Independent*, it was mentioned that there were Indian graves located in the vicinity of the graveyard that were visible for years. This property may once have been part of an earlier burial ground where Native Americans buried their dead. If so, the white man came along and disrespected that space and the dead who had already been laid to rest there. It may be the biggest cliché in ghost lore, but desecrated Native American burial grounds have never been reputed to lead to good things in the future. There were also arrowheads and trinkets uncovered on the property, indicating that a battle with the Indians may have been fought on this land, possibly during the French and Indian War or between opposing tribes. If that is the case, there was violence and bloodshed on this land before it was ever a church graveyard. The cemetery has had a long history of vandalism and desecration, which certainly has not helped matters, though the recent restoration has rectified much of that. What is the root cause of this spirit that has enjoyed terrorizing visitors to the cemetery for generations? Until historical proof emerges, the Man in Black will remain a mystery.

Old Norbourne Cemetery has many legends and strange tales connected to it. There is said to be a tunnel that runs beneath the graveyard into the basement of a house on Queen Street that is part of the ever mysterious underground tunnel system in Martinsburg. Old-timers in town claim there is a secret entrance in the cemetery inside a grave that doesn't contain a body and is marked by a moveable false tombstone that opens onto steps leading down into the tunnel. A Native American historian and descendant of the Tuscarora Indians believes that this tunnel was used by the shamans of the Tuscarora tribe as a place of worship and prayer to keep evil spirits away. They believed caves were portals to the underworld, where evil spirits dwelled.

Next to the cemetery is a small white house that has been the subject of many a spooky tale and urban legend from generations past. The house is part of the Boydville estate, which is located on the other side of the cemetery. The Boydville mansion was constructed in 1812 by Elisha Boyd and was home to many generations of prominent lawyers and politicians. The white house by the cemetery was built in 1851 as a law office for Charles James Faulkner, who resided at Boydville.

Local legends claim the house used to be the residence of the caretaker of the cemetery. One version of the story says that when the Episcopal church was still located in the cemetery and it was an active burial ground, the caretaker resided in the little white house. When the decision was made to move the church to its present location on King Street, he feared the cemetery would close and he would be out of a job. The man went mad and went on a murderous rampage, killing people so that he would still have bodies to bury in the cemetery, securing his job as caretaker. Years later, it is said, a new caretaker moved into the house with his wife. He didn't fare much better: he supposedly hanged himself, and his wife went insane and was committed to an insane asylum. One major flaw of this story involves its timeline. The law office was not built until 1851, and the church was long gone from the cemetery by that point. Plus, while it's a fun story, it sounds like the plot of a bad Vincent Price movie!

Another version of the story places the caretaker and his wife in the house, with five or six large guard dogs that were kept chained up outside. This tale also has the caretaker going around the bend, but this time, the dogs break loose from their chains and are pursued by their owner through the cemetery. When he catches them, he slits every one of their throats and lines them up in the alley that leads to the house from the street. He places their mutilated corpses in running positions as a warning not to approach the house. He then proceeds to go back into the house and murder his wife.

Locals claim that on Halloween night, you can see the misty apparitions of large canines running through the cemetery with chains hanging from their necks. A large, tall man wearing soiled, ragged work clothes chases after them, pursuing them to their bloody end. Many eyewitnesses claim that in one of the upstairs windows facing the cemetery, a woman appears, wearing a high-collar dress with her hair pulled back atop her head in a bun. She looks out over the lonely expanse of markers and monuments with an unhappy expression on her face. Some say she is holding a lit candle. One eyewitness claimed that the woman seemed to be an image on repeat, like a broken record. She would face the window and then turn away, only to repeat the same motions on a continuous loop. Another witness saw only the candle itself moving past the windows.

The house used to have shutters that contained crescent moon cutouts. The shutters would be kept closed. The daughter of a previous caretaker told me that she once saw a pair of eyes staring at her through the crescent moon openings in the closed shutters. Another gentleman said that as a young boy, he was walking past the cemetery early one morning when he saw a pair of female arms hanging out of the shutters of the upstairs window where the ghostly woman appears. He immediately ran home and told his disbelieving grandmother what he had seen. Another longtime resident said that one night, back in the 1950s, he and some friends decided to prop a ladder up against the side of the house and climb in through an open upstairs window to give themselves their own personal tour. When they reached the downstairs level of the pitch-black house, they were met with the sound of the grand piano playing of its own accord. They fled the house, never to return. The same man shared another encounter he and his friends had while hanging out on the vast lawn of Boydville at night. One of the boys needed to use the restroom and ventured into a dark cluster of trees near the law office. Moments later, he came running out, screaming like a banshee. His friends chased him as he fled the Boydville property and ran down the street. The chase lasted for three blocks before they finally caught up to him and got him calm enough to tell them what had happened. He claimed that when he stepped into the thick shadows of the trees, he felt something bump the top of his head. He looked up to see a foot, and as his eyes continued to move upward, he saw that the foot was attached to a leg that was attached to a body that was hanging from the tree above him! The other boys were too afraid to return to see if there was a human body suspended in the trees, and there were no newspaper reports later regarding any dead bodies being discovered on the property. Years later, the man still stood by what he had seen.

People claim to have heard the disembodied growls and barking of dogs that are not present. Rumors also persist of bloodstains that would appear on the walls only to reappear after being painted over. The folklore associated with the creepy little house beside the cemetery has no basis in fact, and archival research reveals nothing out of the ordinary that ever transpired within the house that could have inspired these stories or might explain the many ghostly incidents reported over the years by the locals. Perhaps there was once another structure located on the property where something happened that was the genesis of this story.

Norbourne Cemetery is a strange place. A visit there demands reverence and respect to the many early movers and shakers of Berkeley County history who are interred there. Yet one cannot deny that there is an atmosphere, a vibe that is hard to shake. At times, it almost seems electrified with some kind of spiritual force or an energy that is so thick you feel you could cut it with a knife. It can be a scary place at times. If there is such a thing as a thin place, where the veil between the living and the dead is threadbare, Old Norbourne is certainly one of those places.

CHAPTER 9

SPIRITS OF THE SETTLERS

BUNKER HILL, BERKELEY COUNTY

Colonel Morgan Morgan was born in Wales and educated at Cambridge University. He arrived in America in 1712, and in 1728, he and his family blazed a trail into the Virginia wilderness on land inhabited by Indians. This land was in the area that would become part of Berkeley County in 1772, which became part of the state of West Virginia on November 4, 1863. Colonel Morgan was the builder of the historic landmark, the Morgan Cabin, and can lay claim to being the state's first licensed tavernkeeper and the builder of its first public road. Today, however, he is most famous in the annals of West Virginia history for being the state's first permanent white settler. This area became known for its many mills that were powered by a stream that came to be known as Mill Creek. In 1735, Colonel Morgan acquired a king's patent for one thousand acres on Mill Creek. He divided this among his six sons before he died in 1766.

The present-day Morgan Cabin is believed to be the second home of Colonel Morgan Morgan. Around 1731, he decided to build a more suitable cabin. He selected the present spot because of the large stream nearby. It took about three years to build the cabin. He had to sift sand from the nearby stream to make mud mortar, cut trees in the winter while the sap was down and gather stones for the foundation and the chimney. Between 1976 and 1977, the original cabin was dismantled and rebuilt because the original structure had fallen into such a state of disrepair. The cabin was reconstructed with the use of the original logs that were solid. The whole south wall has the original logs set in place. Today it is a museum filled with artifacts of the period for tourists and visitors to learn the fascinating history of the property and its builder.

The tract of land that Cool Spring Farm is situated on was deeded by Morgan Morgan to his son Zackquill Morgan in 1761. Zackquill built the lovely stone house known as Cool Spring Farm with a log addition on the north side, which was replaced by a frame wing. Zackquill went on to become the founder of Morgantown. The Cool Spring Farm, as it has come to be known, has had many owners and people who have resided within its walls over its very long and rich history. It seems that some of them may remain in spirit.

Pastor Dewey Rowe was invited to stay at the Cool Spring Farm in 2004. He was conducting local pastoral work at the nearby Darkesville Pentecostal Church. During his stay, the pastor decided to sit and relax on the west porch of the home to take in the peaceful scenery and the beautiful landscape. The serene atmosphere was disrupted by what sounded like the piercing scream of a bird. The pastor walked toward the area where he thought the strange sound came from. As he walked toward the old springhouse, he was confronted by a man dressed in a uniform with blood covering the front of him. Shocked and disturbed by what he was seeing, he returned to the house.

Morgan Cabin, home of West Virginia's first permanent white settler. *Courtesy of the Library of Congress.*

Colonel Morgan had six children and several grandchildren, many of whom served in the military during the American Revolution. One grandson, by the name of James Morgan, was a chaplain during the war. While on leave, he returned to the cabin where he and his wife and child were residing at the time. News of his return home reached the Tories. The Tories were colonists who were loyal to the English. They heard about James's return and decided to pay him a most unwelcome visit. What transpired led to a savage and brutal event whose repercussions still resonate to this day. The Tories seized James and brought him to the old springhouse across the road from the cabin. Under the cover of darkness, they bound James's hands and feet and tied him to the springhouse door. A lit candle was held to his chest. His wife and child were forced to watch in horror as seventeen musket balls were fired into his quivering and convulsing body. Can you imagine being made to watch your husband or father executed right before your eyes? This event led to the area being known as Torytown.

Pastor Rowe was not the only person to encounter the blood-soaked apparition of James Morgan. On two occasions, a young girl visited the farm. Both times, she observed and pointed to what she called a man located by the springhouse on the lower north grounds. The child, however, due to her young age and lack of language, was unable to describe what the man was wearing. No one else saw the phantom man. This appears to correspond to the pastor's sighting during his visit to the farm.

About two years ago, I helped establish a Haunted History tour of the Morgan Cabin and grounds in October as a fundraiser for the Morgan Cabin Committee. I conducted the tour the first year. The next year, the committee decided to continue the tours due to the success of the first season. I was not present for that year's tours but was told that one night, while this story was being told, the group of participants saw a shadowy figure dart across the pasture where James Morgan met his demise and where the apparition had previously been seen. This area is farmland, and there was a calf grazing in the field. It must have also seen the ghost, because it began mooing in a distressed manner when the group witnessed the ghostly figure.

As we've discussed in previous chapters, when a tragic event such as James Morgan's execution takes place, it can leave a trace of itself behind, an emotional or psychic residue. Sensitive individuals can usually see or feel these vibrations. The energy that surrounds the site of James Morgan's heinous execution is described as having a strong negative, heavy feeling that penetrates one to the core. Perhaps James, whose life and family were unfairly taken from him in such a grisly fashion, remains there still, clinging to his earthly existence. His, however, is not the only ghost said to roam the Cool Spring property.

A former caretaker at the farm, who worked for the Shingleton family in the early 1990s and for the Hilleary family, reported seeing the specter of a woman in the upstairs hall window on more than one occasion. His sister-in-law felt that someone was watching her when she was in the house and would not go upstairs by herself. The caretaker's wife saw moving shadows when she was in the house. The caretaker himself once felt that someone was behind him in the kitchen. He turned around to see a misty apparition in the middle of the room. He also saw sparks and pops of light outside near the kitchen door. Another relative would not come into the house under any circumstances.

Pastor Rowe experienced many encounters on his visits to the farm. The pastor was a clairvoyant, able to see people and events from the past that others are unable to. He was born with a veil, or caul, over his head; an old superstition states that when this happens, the person will have the special ability to see ghosts.

On the first night of Pastor Rowe's first visit to the farm, he stayed in the Laura Kennedy Trapnell Room. He was restless in bed and saw a shadow pass by the door, in the hall. The pastor got up and followed the shadow into the Walter Scott Kennedy Room, where he saw a woman with her hair wrapped around the top of her head, wearing a black dress. The pastor asked if he could help her. At that moment, a gust of wind blew into the room, and she disappeared. At about the same time, the pastor heard someone wearing high heels walking upstairs. The next day, he carried a small bag to the second floor of the house. He went downstairs, and when he returned, he found that someone or something had rummaged through the bag. The pastor recalled that while trying to communicate with the phantom lady, he had the distinct impression that she had a problem concerning money.

The second night that the pastor slept in the house, he was walking to the bathroom when he again saw the female spirit, standing by the large grandfather clock on the west end of the second-floor hall. She quickly disappeared, and the pastor returned to bed, at which time the grandfather clock chimed once. The clock was not technically operable at the time, nor has the clock ever functioned properly. On hearing the chime, he returned to the hall, where he saw a group of Civil War soldiers rush by the grandfather clock. In addition, a gentleman dressed in clothing from about the middle of the nineteenth century, which included a string tie around his neck, was pressed up against the northwest corner of the hall with an unseen hand holding a saber against his throat. The pastor thought the grandfather clock was somehow associated with Civil War events and asked about the age of the clock. The clock was thought to be from the early nineteenth century; however, the timepiece may have dated to an earlier age.

The pastor was shown a photograph of one of the house's former residents, Mary Quinn Morgan. The pastor seemed to recognize the bun hairstyle worn by Ms. Morgan as well as a ruby or garnet brooch worn by the spirit. Mary Quinn Morgan was born in the Morgan Cabin in 1889 and lived at the Zackquill Morgan house for sixty years. She died in bed in the southeast corner of the Zackquill Morgan Room in 1960. Perhaps she appears as her younger self—as she was when something occurred that keeps her emotionally tied to the house.

The current owner and caretaker of the property has had numerous paranormal experiences of his own. While watching TV in the Walter Scott Kennedy Room, he has seen shadow entities pass in front of the TV screen, followed by one entity that had a pale yellow outline. His former dog used to bark uncontrollably in the Zackquill Morgan Room. The dog would suddenly get up and run out of the house for no apparent reason, as if she were being suddenly probed by unseen hands or feet. The dog would act rather strangely at feeding time, dragging her food across the floor as if being tormented. The dog would eat normally when fed outside on the west porch.

The house has been explored numerous times by paranormal investigators, who have said the house is very haunted. Many photographs taken have revealed strange anomalies, mists and other disturbances.

A lady was driving by the Morgan Cabin at dusk one evening many years ago. She looked at the parking area next to the cabin and saw a Confederate soldier with a musket standing there, staring at her. As she drove past the cabin, she was quite startled to see this person standing there. The figure stood completely still, devoid of movement except for his eyes. She noticed that his eyes seemed to be following her as she passed by him. She drove down to the next intersection and turned around, and when she came back, she looked over at the parking area again. The Confederate soldier was gone. She pulled into the driveway across the road and asked the family who lived there whether they knew if there were any reenactments or special events going on at the Morgan Cabin. They said no; as it was the middle of the week, they didn't know of any special events. Perplexed, the lady replied that she'd seen a Confederate soldier standing in the parking area next to the cabin. The family repeated that they weren't aware of any events. She asked them, "Have you ever seen any ghosts or spirits around the Morgan Cabin?" The family answered, "We are very religious, and we do not believe in such things." The woman drove away very confused about what she had seen.

Why would she have seen the spectral soldier there that fateful evening? Berkeley County was very important to the movements of both the Union and Confederate armies during the three major invasions of the North. Soldiers camped in the Bunker Hill area during the movement of the Army of Northern Virginia toward the fateful showdown at Gettysburg. After the Battle of Gettysburg, the defeated Confederate army's retreat brought a wagon train of wounded through the area. The wagon train, seventeen miles long, carried the bodies of wounded, mangled men. Thousands upon thousands of Confederate troops would camp in and around Bunker Hill, Darkesville and Gerrardstown. The large stream near the cabin was the site of one of their encampments because it was a source of water for the troops. The men would go out in search of food for themselves and their horses. There was no such thing as private property; if they wanted it, they took it. Perhaps the phantom soldier was one of the many wounded brought through the area who didn't survive. Even in death, he still has not given up his post and remains vigilant in his duties, still fighting a war long over.

CHAPTER 10

SPRING MILLS PHANTOMS

SPRING MILLS, BERKELEY COUNTY

It was four o'clock in the morning as Dawn and her husband made their commute to work. Their minds were consumed by thoughts of the day's workload, and the morning thus far had followed their normal routine, as usual. The car traversed the winding curves of Route 901 as it always did every morning. This backcountry road was scenic and gorgeous by day but always seemed lonely and foreboding in the nocturnal hours. The tall, thick trees seemed to form a canopy over the road that obscured the sky from view, and the houses became fewer and farther between. The vehicle came over the bridge just before the crumbling ruins of the old Hammond Mansion. As they navigated a sharp curve near the old stone mill, the couple were met with the sudden, unexpected appearance of a shadow dashing across the road, pursued by the solid figure of a Confederate soldier. As the car made contact with the gray-uniformed figure, he passed through the front of the vehicle, continuing his pursuit of the shadowy figure across the road and toward the small stone house on the right as it melted away into the dark abyss of night. Their hearts pounded with the shock of the near collision and the stinging reality of their dramatic encounter with the unknown. The couple would encounter the spectral Southern soldier many more times in their early morning travels. Another local woman was driving home from a football game with her sister when she, too, had an identical encounter that left her shaken to her soul.

These experiences of locals have been the genesis for a very wildly exaggerated and embellished urban legend over the years, which has included everything from the soldier emerging from a green fog to the vehicle shutting off and the soldier falling on the car and leaving bloody handprints. These details make the story more sensational and dramatic, but the eyewitness encounters themselves are chilling enough without the heavy sprinklings of sugar to sweeten the story.

This area is no stranger to inexplicable happenings. In the late night and early morning hours, mysterious campfires have been seen in the wooded countryside of the desolate hamlet. Nearby, there is a one-lane concrete bridge that spans a gentle, meandering stream. At dusk, some claim, you can hear horses thundering over a long-extinct wooden bridge. Much of the ghostly lore seems to center on the majestic Hammond Mansion, which is the centerpiece of the quaint rural area. The house was built around 1838 by Dr. Allen C. Hammond. Dr. Hammond was born in Frederick, Maryland, and settled in Berkeley County before 1833. He served in the Virginia House of Delegates and as a delegate from Berkeley County during the State Convention in 1861; he voted against secession twice and then changed his vote.

It is believed that Dr. Hammond purchased the property in 1839 from the nephew of Martinsburg's founder, Alexander Stephen. The property included four hundred acres, three dwelling houses, a corn house, a wagon shed, a three-story stone mill and, nearby, a stone distillery, which the doctor kept in operation. George Newkirk "Kirk" Hammond, the doctor's son, was part of the county militia that helped suppress John Brown's raid at Harpers Ferry in 1859, and when the Civil War began, he enlisted in Company B of J.E.B. Stuart's First Virginia Cavalry. He was mortally wounded at the Battle of Yellow Tavern on May 11, 1864. In the fall of 1862, General Thomas "Stonewall" Jackson's men camped here, and in July 1864, Confederate General John McCausland began his raid into Pennsylvania from here.

During the Civil War, Dr. Hammond worked as a surgeon for the Confederate army, and both sides used the house as a hospital. Dr. Hammond's property losses during the Civil War were tremendous. He attempted several times to obtain compensation from the government. He stated that the army had taken ten thousand bushels of corn and fifty barrels of whiskey from his distillery. In addition, they took seventy-five thousand bricks from the kiln; killed his cattle, sheep and hogs; used two crops of wheat and one hundred tons of hay; cut down timber; and took bricks and lumber to build shanties. He estimated that the war had cost him more than $168,000. He received no reimbursement for his losses and was forced to sell the property in 1866. It was purchased by Joseph Duvall for

Hammond House, once used as a Civil War hospital, is one of the most famous haunted houses in Berkeley County. *Author's collection.*

$50,000 and remained in the Duvall family until it was purchased by Max Oates. In 1979, fire gutted the house, leaving a collapsed roof and a burned-out brick shell. The house was later restored to reflect its original grandeur and became a rental property for several years before being sold again; it is now privately owned.

During the time that the house was a rental property, some of the tenants reported strange things. Two ladies who lived there told the property manager that they would sometimes come home from work to find medicine bottles had been removed from the medicine cabinet and neatly laid out, as well as other seemingly childish pranks. Another family had two children who reported some creepy things. One child would consistently say, "Momma, there's a fire in your closet." On another occasion, a child crawled into bed between her mother and her father. Looking across the darkened room, she pointed to a corner and said, "Mommy, who are they?" She wouldn't say anything else about it. About a week later, her brother was the one who climbed into bed and wedged himself between his tired parents. He pointed to the same corner and said, "Who is that?" He also wouldn't divulge any further information when questioned. After that, his mom began looking in that corner on a regular basis but never witnessed anything besides a dark, empty corner. Another family who rented the home had children who complained of having nightmares about the house burning down, and they allegedly captured video footage of ghostly phenomena in the home.

After the fire that destroyed the home in 1979, it sat in ruins for years and became densely overgrown. That was when its ghostly reputation really grew. It became a popular spot for partygoers and thrill-seeking teenagers, and urban legends began to circulate. Some of the stories told have no basis in fact and seem to be nothing more than made-up campfire tales, but there are those who say they've had startling encounters with the other side on this property. It is said that during the Civil War, when the home was used as a field hospital, operations were performed upstairs, and the amputated limbs were thrown from the top window on the right side of the house into a pile to be carted away later. It's been said that a foul stench like that of decomposing flesh manifests on the ground at the corner of the house, as well as a heavy smell of camphor. People claim to have been touched and had their clothing pulled by unseen hands. In the woods behind the house is an old building alleged to have been a slave shack, which people have claimed is thick with an atmosphere of heavy, oppressive energy. Another highly peculiar phenomenon reported is a cold spot no larger than the size of a turkey platter behind the main house. On a hot summer day, people have had the startling experience of stepping into this tiny area, which is always several degrees colder than the surrounding environment.

One night back in the early 2000s, a small group of five curiosity seekers was on a ghost tour of the ruins on an early fall night. The thick woods and overgrown foliage completely obliterated any light that could've seeped through from streetlights or the moon. The empty shell of the structure loomed over them as if it was patiently watching and waiting for them to approach any closer. As the five nervous adventurers watched, they noticed a dim, blue-tinged light beginning to emanate from within the empty shell through the hollow window frames. The longer they watched, the brighter the light became, shining like some kind of ghostly beacon that glowed through every orifice of the once grand antebellum estate. After what seemed like an awe-inspiring eternity, the blue light began to fade and grow dimmer until it completely extinguished itself from view. To this day, I still have no logical explanation for what I witnessed that night. You see, I was one of the five individuals who was present on that long-ago, unforgettable night!

CHAPTER 11
MURDER MOST FOUL
CHARLES TOWN, JEFFERSON COUNTY

The funeral was one of the saddest, most impressive scenes ever seen in Jefferson County. The M.E. Church South was packed from gallery to basement, and hundreds stood on the streets and on the campus of Shepherd College across the way. When the corpse was brought into the church, the scene was extremely touching, and scarcely a dry eye was to be seen. The pitiful moans of the poor mother—"Oh, Susie! Oh, my little girl!"—touched a tender chord and melted even strong men to tears. The coffin was literally blanketed in flowers, and the boys from the Sunday school of the deceased bore rich and beautiful floral arrangements of various forms. The chair usually occupied by the deceased in the choir was tastefully draped in mourning and spoke mutely of a vacancy in that department of church work. The events leading up to this tragic affair had been culminating for several years.

Susie Cameron Ferrell, a popular young woman in the town, was known for her kindness and graciousness. She was in the Methodist church choir, active and well known in the town and most popular with friends and neighbors of all ages. She had many friends and several gentleman callers. At the age of twenty-three, however, she had not made any decisions about marriage. Suzie was friends with Alice Smootz, from another known family of Shepherdstown. Alice had an older brother named Harry. Harry was known as being socially awkward and somewhat peculiar. Susie was kind to him, as she was kind to everyone, and a friendship developed. Unfortunately, Harry misunderstood the nature of their friendship. He asked Susie to marry him, and she refused. After a time, he asked her again. Once again, she refused, explaining that they were friends and to leave it at that. Thus began the relentless stalking and persecution Harry aimed at Susie for the next two years. Wherever she went, Harry dogged her heels. In an attempt to find some peace, she went to visit relatives in Hagerstown, Maryland, but Harry showed up there, claiming he was looking for work. His pleas for marriage continued, and his behavior became more obnoxious. So desperate was Harry for Susie's attention that he began spreading rumors about her, claiming they had been lovers, in hopes that she would marry him to save her reputation. This ploy failed and only served to anger her family.

On a snowy day in January 1892, Susie and her best friend, Lucy Schoppert, were out sledding on New Street. Unbeknownst to them, they were being watched. Susie noticed Harry approaching her and suggested that she and Lucy run to the house of Reverend Neel, a retired Methodist minister, only feet away from where Lucy and Susie were sledding. They did not make it to the house, however, as Harry swiftly caught up with them. Putting Susie in a chokehold, Harry withdrew a .38 caliber pistol and held it to the top of her head. What was said between them no one overheard, but Harry Smootz shot Susie Ferrell point-blank through the skull and brain. It's said that he dropped her body and casually walked away. A hysterical Lucy ran for help, and with the assistance of some neighbors, Susie's lifeless body was taken to the Neel residence.

Harry, meanwhile, retreated to the Entler Hotel, where his brother Charles was enjoying himself at the Globe Tavern there. "I've shot Susie," Harry calmly said, and then he asked Charles, "Should I kill myself?" His brother, shocked, merely said, "I cannot advise you on that." Charles did, however, bring Harry to the house of a neighbor, a dentist named Dr. Stoller, who tried to persuade Harry to turn himself in. At some point, Harry pulled his gun on Dr. Stoller but did not shoot. Out in the streets of Shepherdstown, an angry mob had gathered in pursuit of Harry Smootz. Eventually, he was captured and arrested, but he had to be protected from the angry mob of people set on avenging the death of their beloved town belle. He was brought to Charles Town, the county seat, but had to be taken to Charleston, West Virginia, the state capital, for his own protection.

Harry seemed detached from the whole incident and asked his captors repeatedly, "Is Susie really dead?" When they answered in the affirmative, he muttered, "Lord help us." Harry was sent back to Charles Town for his trial. At first, Harry's attorney attempted an insanity defense, but that was dismissed. Then he attempted to have the case thrown out on a technicality, but that didn't work either. Ultimately, he was charged with the murder of

The Charles Town Post Office, former site of the Jefferson County jail, which housed John Brown and Harry Smootz, who ended his life there. *Author's collection.*

Susie Cameron Ferrell and sentenced to death by hanging. Leading up to the execution, Harry stayed in his bunk much of the time, with his back to the jailors and a blanket over his head. Two weeks before his execution by hanging, Harry was found dead in his cell of a drug overdose. Evidently, Harry's sisters were smuggling morphine to him, first as a liquid and later as pills, which he'd probably stockpiled in his bunk. Harry had taken enough morphine pills to beat the executioner's rope by killing himself.

Susie is buried at the Ferrell family plot in Shepherdstown's Elmwood Cemetery. Ironically, Harry is buried up there too, in an unmarked grave in his family's plot. How ironic that Harry couldn't be close to Susie in life, but here he is eternally close to her in death. The old Jefferson County jail that was located on the corner of George and Washington Streets in Charles Town is long gone, and the post office now occupies that corner. The jail cells in the previous structure are said to have been located where the parking lot is situated behind the post office. People have reported seeing the shadowy figure of a man pacing back and forth in an eight-by-ten space—the size of a jail cell. One eyewitness claimed to have heard the ghostly figure repeatedly vocalizing, "Susie." Could it be that Harry Smootz is haunted by guilt for the heinous murder of the object of his affections? Or perhaps he's contemplating his own mortality as he must've done in the time leading up to his final decision to end his own life.

There are also those who have claimed to hear shots fired and screams on New Street where Susie was gunned down. They've always been heard on January 21, the anniversary of the murder of Susie Cameron Ferrell.

CHAPTER 12
JOHN BROWN'S SOUL GOES MARCHING ON

CHARLES TOWN, HARPERS FERRY, JEFFERSON COUNTY

In 1798, the United States purchased property in Harpers Ferry to build an armory. George Washington chose this site against the advice of a military engineer and two secretaries of war, but the president was considering more than the available water when he insisted the armory be built there. His brother Charles Washington had a great deal of land in Jefferson County, and George owned stock in the Potowmack Canal Company; perhaps they saw an armory at Harpers Ferry as a way of increasing the family's fortune. It was an attitude prevalently shared by the first workers, who believed that the sole purpose of the armory was to supplement their farm incomes. Harpers Ferry also led the way with industrial assembly lines, and it was here that the first interchangeable parts were manufactured at the Hall Rifle Works. No one involved in these early stages of the operation had a clue that the armory would later be thrust into the middle of one of the most harrowing, life-altering events in American history.

John Brown was a fanatical abolitionist who was a veteran of the wars in Kansas. On the night of October 16, 1859, Brown and twenty-one brave men attempted to strike a blow against the evil of slavery. Their purpose was to capture the guns stored in the armory, and they expected that the slaves in the area would join them and, together, they would retreat to the nearby mountains. Using the mountains as their fortress, they would train slaves to use the weapons and make raids deeper into the South to free more slaves. They also expected that the newly freed slaves would join their army. The raiders' purpose was to make it unprofitable for slavery to exist. They hoped to create a separate state in the Shenandoah Valley for the newly freed African Americans. They were determined to hold out against all intruders until the government recognized the rights of all men.

Unfortunately, Heyward Shepherd, a free African American, was the first man killed in the raid. The African Americans who would have joined Brown became disturbed, and the raid was doomed. By noon on October 17, Brown and the remaining raiders were pinned in the fire engine house with their hostages. Firing continued throughout that day. By the morning of October 18, four townspeople had lost their lives and ten of the raiders lay dead. Six raiders were captured and brought to trial in Charles Town. Charged with treason against the Commonwealth of Virginia and inciting slaves to rebel, all were found guilty and sentenced to hang. Five of the raiders had made good their escape.

If John Brown had died during the raid, this attempt might have gone down in history as a minor insurrection. But he lived to be tried, and it was at his trial that he succeeded in placing the whole moral issue of slavery before the world. After his trial, no one could remain neutral on the issue, and eighteen months later, the nation was plunged into a grueling and bloody civil war. John Brown was willing to die for the cause he loved. But does his ghost linger on?

In the late 1970s, tourists visiting Harpers Ferry National Historic Park started noticing an elderly man with a bushy white beard in antique clothing walking the streets of the town. He bore such a striking resemblance to John Brown that visitors assumed he was a reenactor employed by the National Park Service. People would ask him to pose for pictures with them as a memento of their visit to this historic landmark, and he kindly obliged. When the film was developed, the family members were clear, but there was no sign of the bearded stranger, only a blank space where he had posed. Allegedly, thirty to forty of these photos were sent in to the National Park Service by astonished picture takers. I spoke with a lady who personally attested to being one of those who experienced this perplexing phenomenon on a visit to the park in the 1970s with her husband. However, Harpers Ferry is not the only town in Jefferson County with ghostly reverberations of the infamous John Brown raid.

On December 2, 1859, Brown was taken from the Jefferson County jail in Charles Town. He rode atop his coffin, hauled in a wagon, to the gallows. The execution procession traveled to an empty field nearby where a scaffold had been constructed. Among those present at the execution were several individuals who would rise to fame and notoriety in the Civil

Above: The John Brown Fort, located in the lower town portion of Harpers Ferry National Park. *Courtesy of the Library of Congress.*

Left: Infamous abolitionist John Brown is said to haunt several locations in Jefferson County. *Courtesy of the Library of Congress.*

War that would soon commence: future Confederate generals Thomas J. "Stonewall" Jackson, John McCausland and J.E.B. Stuart and the future assassin of President Abraham Lincoln, John Wilkes Booth. Colonel John T. Gibson of the Fifty-Fifth Regiment of the Virginia Militia commanded about eight hundred troops who enforced martial law at the hanging. It is said that John Brown displayed an impressive serenity during his last days and a stern dignity on the scaffold, and he admonished the hangman, "Be quick!" But some accounts claim that he wasn't and that it took Brown a very long time to die. Some thirty-five minutes passed before his pulse ceased. Even then, the soldiers who attended his body were not convinced he was dead. His piercing blue eyes still seemed alive, so the soldiers poured hot wax on them. But this did little good, and witnesses said that Brown's eyes continued to glow with a lifelike luster.

John Brown is said to have been interested in Spiritualism, a popular religion of the Victorian age that was based on séances with the spirits of the dead. While in jail, Brown read a Spiritualist newspaper. It's not surprising that some believe he haunts the location of his death. Colonel Gibson built a beautiful redbrick Victorian mansion on this property in 1891 that stands almost on top of the hanging site. Gibson was a fanatic in the Southern cause who served with distinction in the Confederate army and was presented a Southern Cross of Honor by the United Daughters of the Confederacy. He never really accepted the outcome of the Civil War, which resulted in the Confederate defeat. Not only did Gibson lead the Virginia militia at the hanging of John Brown, but the Jefferson Guards of Charles Town, under Gibson's command, were also the first troops to arrive on the scene at Harpers Ferry, and Gibson led the first armed clash with Brown and his men. In recognition of these services, Gibson received an original copy of John Brown's "Chatham Constitution" (his plan of government if the raid had been successful) as well as the table on which Brown's death warrant was signed. Both items he kept in his stately mansion that he built. For a time after building the house, Gibson produced picture postcards with the hanging site marked by a cross. When the old Jefferson County jail was demolished, John Gibson obtained stones from the building and used them to build a monument to Brown's hanging on the grounds of the property.

Was Gibson dancing on John Brown's grave through these actions? Perhaps he suspected that he might provoke some retaliation from beyond the grave. Every paragraph of the deed to the property begins with the Lord's Prayer. But perhaps the ever combative Brown had the last laugh and struck back. Some say if you go to the house at sunset, you might see Brown's

The Gibson Todd House. John Brown's hanging took place on this property. *Author's collection.*

final agonizing moments. As the shadows deepen, look to the third-story window on the right. It is there that Brown's ghost appears, with his head tilted to the side in the final act of strangulation.

The Jefferson County Courthouse, where Brown's trial took place, still stands today in Charles Town, though it has been expanded and renovated

The Jefferson County Courthouse, scene of John Brown's trial. *Courtesy of the Library of Congress.*

over the years. The jail was located on the southwest corner of George and Washington Streets on a diagonal from the courthouse. During Brown's capture, he was battered with the hilt of a sword. His injuries were slight, but to inflame public feeling in the North, he pretended to be an invalid. He forced his jailers to carry him on a cot every morning from the jail to the courthouse and then reclined on a cot during his trial. According to an old tale passed down by the locals, whenever Charles Town is blanketed in snow, the diagonal from the jail site to the courthouse melts rapidly, before any adjoining roads or sidewalks. No one can account for this strange phenomenon, for there are no heating pipes or other natural causes to explain it. Some people say John Brown's ghost treading back and forth from the jail to the courthouse causes the melted path.

Perhaps there was a bit of prophecy in the lyrics of that old folk ballad by Paul Robeson, "John Brown's Body."

> *John Brown's body lies a-moldering in the grave,*
> *But his soul goes marching on.*

CHAPTER 13

FROM BEYOND THE GRAVES

CHARLES TOWN, JEFFERSON COUNTY

The church steeple towered over the tour group as they entered the historic Zion Episcopal Churchyard that night. Angie and Tim Manuel, along with Kevin Breeden of Charlestown Haunted History Walks, have been conducting ghost walks through the historic district of Charles Town for the past several years. One of the highlights and a favorite stop among tour goers is a nighttime walk through the eerily beautiful graveyard that surrounds the storied church.

Zion Episcopal Church originated as St. George's Chapel, built sometime in the 1770s, which fell into disrepair after the Revolutionary War. The ruins remain on State Route 51, west of Charles Town. The original church located on Zion's present site was built around 1815. A larger church was erected in 1847–48, but soon after its completion, it was destroyed in a disastrous fire. The present structure opened its doors to worshippers on December 6, 1851. During the Civil War, the church was subjected to much abuse by Union troops while it was used as both a barracks and hospital. In the spirit of perseverance, which has been a hallmark of the church throughout its history, the interior walls were replaced, and services continued.

The attached graveyard is a walk through Jefferson County history. There are twenty members of the Washington family buried there who were born at Mount Vernon. Among them are Colonel John A. Washington, the last owner of Mount Vernon, and Lucy Todd Washington, sister of Dolley Madison, who was married to George Steptoe Washington. Additionally,

Zion Episcopal Church. The surrounding churchyard is a museum of Victorian artwork. *Author's collection.*

there are approximately eighty-five to ninety Confederate soldiers buried there, as well as two Revolutionary officers. Those who sleep beneath the earth there have many stories to tell, some inspiring, some heroic and others heartbreaking and tragic, the stories of those whose lives were filled with suffering and despair.

The tour group, led by Kevin, navigated the seemingly endless labyrinth of Victorian-era grave markers beneath the majestic trees that loom over this museum of the dead. The group stopped on the west side of the burial grounds and huddled close as Kevin began regaling them with a story about the notable graves. As immersed as he was in the dramatic tale he was sharing, he couldn't help but notice that some of the participants in the group seemed a bit distracted and were looking toward the stone wall that encloses the churchyard. Their expressions seemed to be changing from curious to awestruck. He finally decided to stop his story and look at whatever was the source of the interruption to his tour. As he glanced between the branches of the adjacent dogwood tree that obscured his view, his eyes were met with a surprise. Walking through the old, weathered dogwood leaves from the previous fall season that had gathered along the stone wall was a shadow. It had no discernible features; it was simply the silhouette of a human figure that was solid black. The shadowy visitor seemed to be aware that Kevin had spotted it; it stopped in its tracks, turned and shot through the cemetery in the direction of the Washington graves, dissolving into the dark recesses of the graveyard. This was not the only encounter with this ethereal being. On another tour, Angie heard disembodied footsteps approaching and caught movement in her peripheral vision as Kevin was telling a story to the group. The apparition made its presence known on three separate occasions. They noticed a strange pattern to these startling manifestations. They always occurred when the tour guides had stopped at one grave and were telling the story of the person interred there: John Yates Beall.

The haunted grave of John Yates Beall. *Author's collection.*

John Yates Beall was born in Jefferson County on January 1, 1835, at Walnut Grove, his family's farm in Charles Town. He was the second of four sons and the fourth of nine children of George Brooke Beall and

Janet Yates Beall. He studied law at the University of Virginia but did not obtain a degree. After his father's death, he took over the management of the farm. Beall was active in the Zion Episcopal Church, and some claim that he was responsible for the construction of the stone wall that borders the churchyard.

John became a private in the Botts Greys, the Charles Town militia company that was on duty for the execution of John Brown. The Botts Greys became Company G of the Second Virginia Infantry, one of the five regiments that composed the Stonewall Brigade. When John was ordered to take a sick soldier to Jefferson County, he learned that Turner Ashby's troops were under attack at nearby Bolivar Heights. Beall joined Ashby and led a charge, in which he was severely wounded in the chest. He later received a medical discharge from the Confederate army and was commissioned an acting master in the Confederate navy. Near Tangier Island in the Chesapeake Bay, Union forces, after months of attempts, captured Confederate raiders, including John Yates Beall, who had damaged a submarine cable, destroyed a lighthouse and captured a Union merchant ship carrying supplies. John was later returned to Richmond as part of a prisoner exchange. He refused a commission in the Confederate secret service and went to Canada to resume his raiding activities. John and nineteen men disguised themselves as civilian passengers to seize a ferry on Lake Eerie. They aborted their plan to capture a Union gunboat and free Confederate prisoners when another group of Confederate agents was apprehended. John was captured at Niagara Falls during an attempt to derail trains carrying Confederate prisoners. He was imprisoned in New York, where he was tried and convicted as a spy. Despite a petition for his pardon signed by ninety-two members of the U.S. Congress, John Yates Beall was hanged and buried in New York on February 24, 1865. His last words were, "I protest against this execution. It is absolute murder—brutal murder. I die in the service and defense of my country." His body was reinterred in the Zion Episcopal Church graveyard in Charles Town on March 22, 1870.

John Yates Beall, hanged as a spy during the Civil War. *Courtesy of the Library of Congress.*

There are also stories told of people seeing a man near John Yates Beall's tombstone wearing a suit and a bow tie with a goatee—closely resembling photographs of him. Allegedly, he appears for only an instant but long enough to startle those who see him because his head is tilted to one side, resting on his shoulder as if his neck is broken. I cannot vouch for the authenticity of these encounters as I've never spoken to eyewitnesses who claim to have seen him in this particularly ghastly form. But he is not the only spirit in this history-rich graveyard.

George Washington Turner was one of the most prominent and influential citizens of Jefferson County. He was born on January 11, 1813, the son of Henry Smith Turner and Catherine Blackburn Turner. He was an 1831 graduate of the United States Military Academy. After graduation, he became assistant professor of mathematics at the academy. From 1832 to 1836, he served in the United States Army in South Carolina, North Carolina and the Florida Wars. After his wartime service, he resigned his commission and returned to Jefferson County. After his father's death, he inherited part of Wheatland Plantation, the family farm, located five miles south of Charles Town. He spent much of his life as a farmer and was respected and honored by his fellow citizens and loved by his servants. He was a brave and generous man known for his strict honesty and unblemished honor.

On October 17, 1859, George heard about the John Brown insurrection at Harpers Ferry. He immediately ordered his horse and gun brought to him by his favorite servant and headed to the scene. He entered the Ferry through the town of Bolivar, riding over Camp Hill and down High Street. As he rode leisurely along, the inhabitants warned him of the danger he was approaching. He listened but still rode on. Passing down High Street, he stopped and dismounted near its intersection with Shenandoah Street, in front of the house of Captain Moore. He was standing by the door, resting his musket on a board fence and preparing to take aim at one of the raiders when a bullet from a Sharp's rifle struck him in the shoulder—the only part of him that was exposed. The ball, after taking an eccentric course, entered his neck and killed him almost instantly. A physician who examined the body described the wound as being of the strangest kind, the bullet having taken a course entirely at variance with the laws supposed to prevail over such projectiles. It was thought by many that the shot had not been aimed at Mr. Turner and that the man who fired it was not aware of him being nearby. There were two men named McClenan and Stedman in the middle of the street opposite Captain Moore's house. They had guns in their hands, and one of them, we may suppose, fired the shot that proved fatal to Mr. Turner. The funeral of George Turner was a solemn and affecting affair.

The military were all under arms and attended in a body. Perhaps no one was impacted by his tragic death more than his sister Mary Allibone.

Mary Elizabeth Blackburn Turner Allibone was the first child of Catherine Blackburn and Henry Smith Turner. She was born in 1798 in the Blackburn family home, Rippon Lodge, in Virginia. As a young child, Mary was sent to live with her grandparents Colonel Thomas and Christian Blackburn. The tragedies in Mary's life began with the death of her and George's mother in 1817 during the birth of their sister Catherine. Mary married Thomas Allibone of Philadelphia, Pennsylvania, at a young age. Allibone was a graduate of the University of Pennsylvania with a law degree. Their happiness, however, was short-lived; he died at age thirty-four on August 1, 1821, of insanity, leaving Mary a widow at age twenty-three. Following the death of her husband, Mary returned to the family home, Wheatland, in West Virginia. Her and her brother George's father died in 1834, and their stepmother, Lucy Lyons Turner, was often away from Wheatland, leaving Mary to run the family home.

Mary never overcame the devastating loss of her beloved brother George, and her mental health severely declined. She sank into the deepest, blackest

The Turner family plot, where Mary Allibone is said to still mourn the loss of her beloved brother. *Author's collection.*

mourning. Shortly after his death, she was taken to Mount Hope Lunatic Asylum in Philadelphia, Pennsylvania. For the last few months of her life, she continued to sink until her broken spirit burst its earthly bonds and returned to its maker on March 6, 1860, at sixty-one years of age—a sad sequel to the senseless, premature death of her brother. Mary is buried beside her brother in the Turner family plot at Zion Episcopal Church. The inscription on her tombstone reads:

> *December 26, 1798*
> *And departed of this*
> *life March 6, 1860*
> *of grief for the loss of*
> *her dearly beloved*
> *brother by whom*
> *she sleeps*
> *of too gentle*
> *and loving a nature*
> *bear the rough things of*
> *earth when the*
> *tempest of grief*
> *passed over her*
> *she yieldeth the*
> *immortal spirit of ending*
> *rest and shelter in the*
> *Savior's bosom*

Late at night, locals claim to have seen a woman dressed in black Victorian mourning attire. She wanders around the Turner family plot, wringing her hands and sobbing inconsolably, crying out, "George," repeatedly, causing those who witness the heartbreaking scene to feel her gut-wrenching anguish. Even in death, Mary is still eternally grieving the loss of her beloved brother.

CHAPTER 14
THE CHOP SHOP

SHEPHERDSTOWN, JEFFERSON COUNTY

The weather the day of the battle was unseasonably hot. Many soldiers in both armies died from exhaustion during the terrific struggle, with not a wound found on their bodies. The engagement began at daybreak with an artillery duel. The thunder of the cannon awoke the people of Shepherdstown, and there were many sorrowing hearts among the women and older folks, for their sons and husbands and brothers were in the battle. The tide of wounded began to flow into the town early that morning.

The bloodiest single-day battle in American history was the Battle of Antietam, on September 17, 1862, which occurred in the nearby town of Sharpsburg, Maryland. There were twenty-three thousand casualties in a twelve-hour period. All through the day, the bloody stream of mangled and wounded soldiers flowed into Shepherdstown, and all day long could be heard the fury of the battle and musketry discharges. Some of the soldiers were stragglers who were getting away from danger, some were the wounded who were able to walk and look after themselves and up to eight thousand badly wounded soldiers in need of immediate attention were brought in by ambulances. All the soldiers were hungry and thirsty, and many were exhausted by the time they reached Shepherdstown. There was always a crowd around the town pumps, which were kept going continuously. Some of the men, fevered by their wounds and almost perishing from thirst, could hardly drink enough to be satisfied. The women of the town tore their petticoats to be used as bandages and worked tirelessly day and night aiding the wounded with food and care.

Almost every church, home, business, barn and warehouse—and any place that could hold a body—was used as a field hospital or infirmary. Wounded soldiers were laid out in the yards and streets. The town's iconic and majestic McMurran Hall was still under construction, and there was scaffolding all around it. Straw was placed on the planks, and bodies were laid out all over the scaffolding. The wounded were in dire need of immediate attention; many of them were bleeding to death or had lead poisoning. The only way to save them was to amputate the affected limb. The second floor of the old Moulder Hall building on the southwest corner of King and German Streets was used as headquarters for these emergency surgeries. The surgeons labored endlessly over the mangled and maimed Confederates. Severed appendages were thrown out of the second-story windows of the building into carts, wagons and corncribs below. The limbs were then buried somewhere or dumped into the Potomac River. What a nightmarish scene it must've been.

Today, the old Moulder Hall building is a delightful café and bakery known as the Sweet Shop. The delicious German pastries served there are much sweeter than the building's gruesome and gory past. For years, in this building, disembodied voices have been heard and shadowy figures have been seen. Employees of the Sweet Shop have seen things falling from the second floor, past the windows in the back, and have felt like someone has brushed past them. Employees have claimed that phantom conversations have been heard, as well as the sounds of activity in empty rooms. On the second floor of the building are apartments where a woman has been seen going from room to room checking on the occupants, the way a nurse would check on her patients. Outside of the building, a woman has been seen sweeping the sidewalk very early in the morning.

Some have seen the apparition of an older man, dressed as a Civil War officer, who has been nicknamed the Colonel. Interestingly, he has been seen wearing a gray uniform by some and a blue uniform by others. He is usually standing in one area of the first floor of the building and has been seen walking through a wall. There were doorways on the first floor at one time that have since been bricked over.

Who is the Colonel? There are several theories. One theory is that he is Dr. Alexander Tinsley, the attending surgeon associated with the building after the Battle of Antietam. However, it is unlikely that it is he, because he was only thirty years old when he served as chief surgeon in Shepherdstown, and the Colonel is seen as an older man. Dr. Tinsley moved to Baltimore and lived out the rest of his life there. He is buried in Shepherdstown, but I see no

The Sweet Shop bakery was once used as a Civil War hospital where many amputations took place. Bones are said to have been recovered on the property. *Author's collection.*

reason why he'd be haunting the town, unless even in death he cannot give up his appointed post and responsibility.

As mentioned, the building was originally called Moulder Hall, named after William Moulder, who was the postmaster of Shepherdstown in the 1850s. He died in 1863, and though there is no evidence that he was a soldier, as postmaster he likely would have had a uniform of some sort. Perhaps it is he who keeps an eye on his building and the activities therein.

There is another theory. Perhaps the Colonel is what is known as residual energy. Residual energy is not the spirit or soul of a person. It is more like an energetic snapshot or piece of film that is imprinted where a traumatic or otherwise emotionally charged event occurred. It is a scenario that is repeated over and over, such as an apparition of a man walking through a wall. After the Battle of Antietam, Confederate General Robert E. Lee retreated across the Potomac River and encamped a couple of miles outside of Shepherdstown. It's highly likely that Lee rode into town to check on the welfare of his soldiers. The Colonel has been seen wearing gray and, at other times, wearing blue. Before Robert E. Lee joined the Confederacy, he served with the Union army of the Potomac. Could the gray haired gentleman known as the Colonel be the residual energy of the famous Robert E. Lee?

CHAPTER 15

THE GHOST OF IDA SNYDER

SHEPHERDSTOWN, JEFFERSON COUNTY

Harry Snyder was the owner and editor of the *Shepherdstown Register*. The *Register* was a prodigious newspaper that was published for over one hundred years. In the late 1800s, Harold built a beautiful house on the main street of Shepherdstown for his growing family. Serpentine stone from Pennsylvania was used for the façade of the house, and the structure was further enhanced by a large front porch. It is now the offices for Trinity Episcopal Church.

Harry and Ida Snyder had five children, and their daughter Rachel, known as Ray-Ray, was said to have "the sight"; that is, she was a psychic. Ray-Ray was a lovely dark-haired girl with large, intense eyes. In the summer of 1907, when she was around twelve years old, something began to trouble her. She felt that Death followed her everywhere and that she needed to keep it out of the house. She would quickly enter and exit the house, shutting the door tightly behind her, and tried to keep the family from venturing out. She would want the shutters closed and the doors barred. But no one paid much attention to a twelve-year-old's imagination. This ominous foreshadowing tormented the worried child for a week.

It was a warm summer day on July 28, 1907, when Ida and her brood got in their carriage and headed the few blocks to the Lutheran church, where her husband was already waiting. As they were turning from German Street left onto King Street, something went wrong: a strap broke on the horse's harness. And as they went to make the turn, something jolted the horse. Mother Ida, for what reason we will never know, appeared to try to get out of the moving carriage. Ray-Ray grabbed at her mother's belt, but it was too tight, and she couldn't grasp it. Whether her foot got caught or her skirt got entangled, Ida Snyder fell from the carriage and hit her head with such force that her neck was broken and a large blood vessel in her neck ruptured. Churchgoers quickly ran to her aid, and she was carried to a nearby house, but she never regained consciousness. Just as quickly as that, the Snyder children lost their mother and Harry was left a widower. It was one of the most distressing occurrences to have ever happened in Shepherdstown. Ida was forty-six years of age, and few people had ever lived in Shepherdstown who were more sincerely loved. She was active in her church, sympathetic and charitable to the poor and kind and gracious to all, and her death was a dreadful shock and a great loss to the whole community.

After that fateful summer, Rachel continued to have the gift of foreknowledge for the rest of her life. She became a teacher and was much loved by her many nieces and nephews and known for her playful nature. Rachel and the rest of the family are buried in Shepherdstown's Elmwood Cemetery. In life, Ida was not always happy at the Snyder home. She originally came from Philadelphia, and Shepherdstown probably seemed like isolated country to her. To ease her lonely, homesick feelings, her husband had the Pennsylvania serpentine stone put on the house, making it the only green house in town. His efforts must've made Ida feel more at home, because Ida's spirit remains in the family home in Shepherdstown, not in Pennsylvania.

Since the time of Ida's death, people who have lived in the house have felt a presence and seen the apparition of a woman in a light-colored dress. In the 1960s, a family lived in the home with five children. The oldest daughter and the next-to-youngest son both witnessed a headless woman in a long white dress standing on the second-floor landing of the main staircase of the home. Perhaps the spirit of Ida Snyder was trying to shield the children from the ghastly sight of her crushed head by appearing without it. To others, however, Ida has appeared as she was before the tragic buggy wreck: with a warm, smiling countenance. She has been seen many times, often by children, both inside and outside the house. Often, people notice the scent of some Victorian perfume or the smell of flowers when entering the house. They've also experienced doorknobs turning and rocking chairs rocking unassisted when no one is nearby. Another occupant of the home heard footsteps walking across the upstairs when she was alone. In a much stranger experience, the same woman was looking at her reflection in a mirror when she realized that the room contained an

The Snyder Home. Ida Snyder is said to have haunted the family home since her tragic death. *Author's collection.*

additional person—there was a man wearing a bowler hat standing behind her. Who could this additional spirit be? Harry Snyder lived for almost thirty years after the death of his beloved wife. As far as anyone knows, he never thought of remarrying. He died on May 17, 1935, at seventy-three years of age. Not all ghost stories have tragic endings where spirits are earthbound due to bitterness and anger, unable to let go because they are consumed by vengeance against injustice in life. Perhaps Harry and Ida, reunited in spirit, live on for eternity, sharing their home and their love together in the afterlife.

CHAPTER 16

THE DUEL

SHEPHERDSTOWN, JEFFERSON COUNTY

It was a quiet Sunday afternoon when Dana visited the Historic Entler Hotel Museum at the corner of Princess and East German Streets. There were no other visitors present on this occasion. She admired the dining and sitting chambers with their antique furnishings downstairs. She glanced curiously at the books in the main hallway about Shepherdstown and its unique history and the people who helped shape it. She then climbed the beautiful staircase that led to the second floor of the building, anticipating the curiosities and treasures it held. Upon reaching the top, she walked down the long hallway and came to a type of alcove. Suddenly things felt very closed in, and she felt a claustrophobic sensation creep over her. Sounds within the empty building were amplified and became very loud. The faucet in the nearby bathroom began to drip with a reverberating echo. All sorts of creaking and other noises came from the empty rooms at an unusually high volume. At this point, she faintly heard a man's voice call, "Mother, Mother."

In 1796, Phillip Entler purchased land from Christian Cookus and built a brick structure. This structure burned down in the famous Shepherdstown fire of 1912, but the foundation remains. Christian Cookus also built a two-story building on the east side of Entler's property, and then a man named Daniel Bedinger bought the remaining portion of the lot and built a three-story brick structure. Eventually, the properties were sold to James Brown and Edward Lucas, and in 1824, Daniel Entler, grandson of Phillip, acquired them. Over the centuries, these buildings have served as a home, a hotel, a

The Entler Hotel is said to be home to many spirits, most famously an ill-fated duelist. *Author's collection.*

tavern, a field hospital, a men's dormitory for Shepherd College, lodging for U.S. Navy and Air Force cadets attending Shepherd College during World War II and apartments. Today the Entler Hotel serves as the Shepherdstown Museum, the Shepherdstown Historical Society and business offices.

One story from the building's rich past has had a very long shelf life, permanently woven into the fabric of the town's folklore. In 1809, two young men, Peyton Smith and Joseph Holmes, were at an establishment known as the Barracks in Winchester, Virginia. They were not the best of friends but rather acquaintances who were part of the same social circle of friends. On this occasion, a disagreement had arisen between the two men, and Joseph Holmes had given Peyton Smith repeated causes of irritation. Despite Smith's efforts to get Holmes to desist, Holmes persisted in being obnoxious. As a result, Smith called Holmes a "damned fool!" Things escalated into a fistfight, and demands were made. Goading friends challenged Holmes to defend his honor in a way that only a duel could achieve. Dueling was an arranged engagement in combat between two people with matched weapons. It was based on a code of honor. Duels were fought not to kill the opponent but to gain "satisfaction"—that is, to restore one's honor by demonstrating a willingness to risk one's life for it. So Joseph Holmes challenged Peyton Smith to a duel, to be held on the banks of the Potomac River on the Maryland side. Peyton Smith did not want to duel; nor did he want to fight. He was a gentle person, by all accounts, and very close to his mother. One might say he was a bit of a mama's boy. Smith reached out to a family friend, Dr. Grayson, asking him to try to talk Joseph Holmes out of dueling, but Holmes refused, for he had a score to settle. He wanted Smith to apologize and to admit to being a liar for calling him a "damned fool." Perhaps it was pride, but Smith refused to do this.

In the early morning hours one day in November 1809, the resigned Peyton Smith left his Winchester home for Shepherdstown. The duel was to be fought on the Maryland side of the Potomac River because Virginia was beginning to frown upon dueling and Shepherdstown, at that time, was probably the closest Virginia town to the Maryland border. People had gathered on the banks of the Potomac to witness the event. Back in Winchester, Peyton's mother got wind of what was happening and frantically headed for Shepherdstown. It has been said that Peyton didn't even reach for his pistol. Joseph Holmes fired, and the bullet mortally struck Peyton Smith. There are those who claimed that Holmes had been trying to shoot over Smith's head, but if that was so, he must not have taken aim very well.

Peyton Smith was brought across the Potomac and taken to room 1 of the Entler Hotel. As Peyton's body was being carried to the hotel, he repeatedly called out for his mother. "Mother, Mother," he cried. "Has my mother come?" He wailed in this fashion until he lost consciousness and his spirit left his body. His hysterical mother arrived soon after only to be struck by the crushing blow of the reality that she was too late to stop her son from engaging in the duel that would claim his life. Her beloved son had passed alone, without her by his side. If she had arrived sooner, she might have been able to stop this tragic turn of events. The guilt and heartbreak were like a sharp dagger piercing the very core of her soul. The devastated woman took her son's lifeless body back home to Winchester. This was one of three duels that finally drove the State of Virginia to pass an anti-dueling law. As for Joseph Holmes, there were no legal consequences for him. Dueling was still an acceptable method of settling a dispute, and Holmes's father was a judge. Peyton Smith and Joseph Holmes were no more than twenty years old—no older than the students who presently attend Shepherd University.

Over the years, volunteers and visitors to this building have reported hearing a man's voice faintly calling for his mother. Moans and footsteps are heard, and objects get moved around. The exact location of room 1 is not known, but one room is said to hold a strange energy that many have felt. To some, it feels very cold and oppressive, and in this room, it is said, the bed will be found disheveled, the covers and pillows thrown about. One evening, three friends passed this building. Looking through the windows, they could see a shadowy figure on the stairway leading to the second floor. Attempts to take a picture were fruitless, as the screens on their digital cameras would just go blank. Peyton Smith is believed to have some spectral company on the astral plane that coincides with the living within these walls. Some have reported seeing the apparition of a young girl in the upper windows. A psychic once entered the room where the girl has been seen in the windows and saw the child. She said she was hiding there for fear of being punished. The cause of the Great Shepherdstown Fire of 1912 remains unknown; however, the psychic felt the young girl possibly caused the fire through playing with matches. One visitor claimed to have seen a man in a brown coat pass quickly by a doorway on the second floor. A woman in gray is seen in the vestibule on the first floor, and a more lavishly dressed woman has been seen in the hallway. A docent at the museum believes there are at least twenty-two spirits that inhabit this ancient building. Centuries of history and so many people have been in and out of those buildings; surely, it holds many secrets and memories.

CHAPTER 17
A HAUNTING ON NEW STREET
SHEPHERDSTOWN, JEFFERSON COUNTY

Rachel Snyder had just been widowed—her husband was tragically killed in the Civil War—and she was struggling financially. She had five children to raise, and she was desperate to cut expenses and find a more affordable home in which to raise her family. Rachel heard that there was a house available for rent and the rent was cheap. The house was part of Stone Row, located on New Street in the quaint little village of Shepherdstown. Stone Row is made up of four houses. It had its origins as a brewhouse; Phillip Shutt built the original one-story limestone structure in about 1792. In the 1800s, a second story of brick was added to the structure, and it was divided into separate living spaces. The second story was originally housing for the Irish workers on the C&O Canal.

Rachel's friends warned her that the house she was interested in was haunted and urged her not to make the move. Several families had already moved out of the place in terror, claiming that it was possessed of all manner of things that go bump in the night and occurrences too dreadful to speak of. But Rachel had more worrisome matters to think of than vexing spooks, so she moved her family in.

Shortly after they took up residence in the house, they got some wood for the kitchen stove, which was in the cellar. After they sawed the wood, they stacked it in a small basement room adjoining the kitchen and put the sawhorse and saw up on top of the wood pile. While they were sitting upstairs one night, they heard the woodpile crash to the stone floor, along with the terrible racket of the saw and the sawhorse hitting the ground.

Stone Row was once besieged by terrifying poltergeist activity that was linked to rumors of scandal and murder. *Author's collection.*

Rachel was too tired to bring herself to get up and go downstairs to put things back in order. The next morning, it came as quite a surprise when the family ventured downstairs to find everything in place, exactly as they had left it before hearing the terrible commotion the night before. This incident was only the beginning of the supernatural harassment that was about to torment this family.

Often, when the family was upstairs, they would hear utensils, skillets, pots and pans banging to the floor from the nails in the kitchen walls that held them. On investigation, nothing was ever out of place. In another room, books were heard falling from shelves, furniture was thrown about and china and glass were smashed—until the very instant they threw open the door. Immediately, all would be still, and every article would be in its proper place. Sometimes, mocking disembodied laughter would be heard. In the stillness of midnight, the *tip-tap* of a woman's footsteps could be heard, and the *swish* of silk skirts was plainly audible as she stepped softly about the place.

One Sunday morning, Rachel and her two older daughters had gone to church. The younger three were left at home. The young son was enjoying a book when he heard footsteps coming up from the cellar. The door at the top of the cellar stairs was locked, but the footsteps came right through the locked door and started down the hall toward the living room. The other two children bolted from the house, but the little boy, paralyzed with fear, clutching his little book, didn't budge from the chair. The footsteps drew closer and closer until they were just outside of the living room. The child trembled in anticipation of the entry of the invisible intruder, but the footsteps stopped. Rachel would try to rationally explain away the noises to the children, but they were terrified, and when the youngest son knelt beside his bed to say his prayers at night, he wondered if he would ever be able to pray without being afraid.

Late one night, Rachel was awakened by neighbors pounding on her front door, insisting that there was a fire in the cellar; they had seen the flames through the basement windows. Rachel explained that the fireplace in the kitchen was not in use, but the neighbors persisted. Finally, she invited them to come into the house and inspect the basement for themselves—only to find the fireplace as cold as death.

The most disturbing and persistent of the audible manifestations that besieged the home was the feeble cry of a baby. It would start in an upper room and travel down the staircase to the first floor and then go up the main hall to the cellar steps down to the kitchen. In the far corner of the dank room beyond the cellar kitchen, it would begin to fade away as it sank into the earth, growing fainter and fainter until at last there was but a heartrending gasp, as if the last breath had been smothered in its throat. This gut-wrenching scenario played out continuously, eliciting both sympathy and horror in all those who heard the phantom baby.

The neighbors were very sympathetic and helpful toward Rachel and her family and the constant onslaught of the paranormal maelstrom. At one point, they decided to band together and wage spiritual war against the unseen tormentors. They got a bell, a book and a candle and went to every room in the house, intoning, "In the name of the Father and of the Son and of the Holy Ghost, who are you and what do you want?" The ritual failed to bring any relief to the desperate and terrified family. One day, as the activity reached a crescendo, Rachel snapped. She flung open the door of the living room and defiantly shouted down the hall, "What in the devil do you want?" The noises suddenly ceased, and all was quiet for two weeks.

One summer, an aunt came to visit from her home in Emmitsburg, Maryland. The noises ceased on her arrival but soon recommenced with a vengeance. The aunt realized quickly that something was terribly wrong with the little house at Stone Row. She was of the Catholic faith and decided that it was time to bring out the spiritual big guns. She contacted Father Hickey, her priest, and he promised to do what he could from afar. Whatever he did, it seemed to finally bring peace to the household. The frightening storm of supernatural manifestations came to an end, and the noises were never heard again. There were many attempts to solve the mystery of the bewitched dwelling and discover the cause of the many disturbances. Old folks in the town hinted at trouble that occurred there and whispered of a tragedy they were afraid to speak of openly.

During the Civil War, a married couple, John and Mary Harrington, lived in the house that was later occupied by Rachel Snyder and her children. To make ends meet, they decided to rent out a portion of their home to a young man named Wesley Culp. Wesley was born and raised in Gettysburg, Pennsylvania, and was a wheelwright for a wagonmaker named Hoffman. He came to Shepherdstown in the 1850s when Hoffman moved from Gettysburg and opened a wagon shop on Princess Street. Mary and John became fast friends with their new boarder—especially Mary, who became Wesley's mistress.

When the Civil War came, John and Wesley enlisted in Company B of the Second Virginia Infantry Regiment. At the Battle of Antietam, John and Wesley were captured by Union forces and taken to the Union's prisoner of war camp at Fort McHenry, Maryland. They were offered privilege of parole, which has a special meaning in military law: a prisoner of war is given freedom after promising never again to take up arms. John and Wesley both wrote home to Mary to ask her advice. Mary returned a letter to each. To her husband, she advised, "You were born in the South. You have lived in the South throughout your whole life. Swearing to that oath would be living a lie. Rot in prison, but don't sign the oath." However, to Wesley, she wrote, "You were born in the North. You have family in the North. Swear the oath, kiss the book and hurry on home." Both men followed Mary's advice.

While her husband rotted in jail, Wesley and Mary kept each other company. A while later, the neighbors saw Mary was visibly pregnant. The town gossips began wagging their tongues, for they knew that Mary's husband had been gone far too long for him to have been the father. Wesley, it seemed, did not take to the idea of fatherhood, and oath or not, he signed up again to fight for the Confederacy and went off to war again. Wesley fought in several battles until he was shot and killed at Gettysburg, on his own family's land, Culp's Hill.

Back in Shepherdstown, many months went by, and Mary stayed secluded in her house on Stone Row. When she finally began socializing in the town again, she was not pushing a baby carriage. She was as slim as ever and behaved as if there had never been a pregnancy, never been a baby. No one, in fact, ever saw Mary's baby. Years later, Rachel Snyder and her children as well as other witnesses heard a baby crying upstairs and being taken to the cellar, where the crying ceased. Could this have been a ghostly reenactment of an event that took place? Did Mary commit the unspeakable act of murdering her baby by smothering it and burying it in the dirt floor of the kitchen basement?

It is not known what happened to Mary's husband, John, but years later, when Mary was on her deathbed, succumbing to cancer, her last words were a scream, over and over: "I am sinking into hell! I am sinking into hell!"

Whatever the truth may be, there are some to this day who say you can still hear the muffled cries of a newborn baby coming from the subterranean stairs beneath Stone Row.

CHAPTER 18

WILL THE REAL GHOSTS OF SHEPHERD UNIVERSITY PLEASE STAND UP?

SHEPHERDSTOWN, JEFFERSON COUNTY

When exploring the ghostly legends of Shepherdstown, mention must be made of the many spirits that share the dormitories and buildings with students on the Shepherd University (formerly college) campus. These stories are well known and have been covered in many other collections and websites concerning West Virginia ghosts. However, many of the stories you've probably heard or that have appeared in previous publications have many erroneous facts and far-fetched backstories—and in the case of some of the tales, parts of the narratives have been proven false. In this chapter, I present the most accurate versions of the stories culled from the available records and resources. There is no doubt that students and faculty have had paranormal experiences, but the stories handed down through generations to explain their origins look very questionable when stacked against the facts.

McMurran Hall

The clock tower building known as McMurran Hall was built on the former site of the home of Shepherdstown's founder, Thomas Shepherd. The French and Indian War was going on in Shepherd's time, and he built a rather large fort/stockade on this property to protect the settlers of the town.

McMurran Hall. Initially constructed as a courthouse, it is one of the most iconic buildings of the Shepherd University Campus. *Author's collection.*

His children, grandchildren and great-grandson, Resin Shepherd, were all born here. The clock tower building was originally intended to be a town hall. Resin Shepherd began construction on it in 1859. After construction was completed, it served as the Jefferson County Courthouse for five years. During the Civil War, when Charles Town was ravaged, the Jefferson County seat was moved to Shepherdstown. When the county seat was returned to Charles Town, they had this large, beautiful building that they didn't know what to do with, so a committee decided to start a college. It was started in 1871, and in 1872 it was chartered as a state normal school—that is, a school for teachers.

To the right of McMurran Hall is where a metaphysical phenomenon known as an energy vortex is said to be present. A vortex is said to be a concentration of the Earth's energy that comes forth, and where these highly charged areas are located, people are naturally drawn to build their temples, cathedrals and schools of higher learning. These are areas where people may feel their intuitive abilities increase, or they may simply perceive a feeling of calm.

A vortex is said to manifest when a ley line and a geodetic line intersect and it is strengthened by waterways. Ley lines are thought to be pathways or lines of psychic or spiritual force, magnetic or possibly gravitational in nature, that follow the course of deeply buried waterways and form a grid across the Earth's surface. Studies have revealed that there is a geodetic line that runs exactly along the town (water) run. At the spot next to McMurran Hall, a ley line, a geodetic line and the limestone-lined town run all intersect. This information was supplied by maps and measurements provided by an engineer. The vortex energy is also felt in this area. Often people feel tingly, dizzy energy—or feel nothing. Since a vortex comes forth as a flow, these sensations could be part of the vortex—or it could be another, as there are said to be several in Shepherdstown.

A vortex is also where spirit activity may increase. Interestingly, there is an old legend connected with McMurran Hall. Generations have claimed that at night, a man can be seen peering down from the top of the clock tower at passersby. Legend says it's the ghost of a soldier who died there; he hides up there because he likes to be left alone and people rarely go up there. Some say it's Thomas Shepherd himself, still looking out over his town. Of course, it could be something people have seen after late-night visits to the town pubs!

Knutti Hall

The building behind the clock tower is Knutti Hall. It stands on the site where the original Normal Building was located. A boiler explosion caused a fire that burned the building down after only five years. No one was killed, but people claim to have smelled smoke, heard footsteps running down the halls and doors slamming and seen the apparition of a woman with a burned face.

Turner Hall

There is a ghost by the name of George who is said to haunt the Rock Room in the basement of Turner Hall. The tales allege that George was a construction worker when Turner was being built who died in an accident. Some versions of the story add that he landed on the rocks when he plunged to his death and the decision was made to build the residence hall around the rocks that surrounded the worker's body rather than removing it. Legend says this is why the building does not have an official basement but rather a rock bottom instead. In any event, since this was the site of his death, he haunts the building. This story has never been proven, and there are no facts supporting the validity of this fatal accident. But whether it's George from the legend or someone else, a presence seems to like to play tricks on people by turning televisions on—and back when VCRs were still a thing, it would rewind and fast-forward video tapes at all hours of the night. Others claim that they have had problems with objects in their room being moved, such as posters being turned upside down and stuffed animals being repositioned. One student who used to live in Turner Hall said that in one incident, she and her roommate were experiencing problems with their stereo. As they went to turn it off, it shut itself off, the lid to the player opened and the CD shot out and shattered against the wall.

Kenamond Hall

The resident ghost of this dormitory is a little boy about eight years of age who wears knickers, a vest and a driving cap. He was supposedly the son of a maintenance worker. It's said that he was playing, patiently waiting for his father to finish work so that he could take him swimming. His father kept telling him that it would have to wait. Eventually, the boy went swimming on his own and did not survive the Potomac. There is an obvious hole in this version of the story that renders it implausible. Kenamond Hall was not dedicated as a residence hall until 1966. The little boy is most definitely not dressed in 1960s attire. He looks like he's from the nineteenth or early twentieth century, so it's not possible for his father to have been a maintenance worker there in the late '60s, when the dormitory was built. Yet another version of the story states that the boy was standing near the construction site where one of the bridges from Shepherdstown to Sharpsburg was being built. He was waiting for his father, who was on the river. While waving to his father below, he fell to his death.

Again, neither version of this story has been proven true, but Kenamond Hall has been haunted by a spectral male child for many years. He enjoys watching television, so he likes to go from room to room and turn TVs on, tuning them to cartoons. He also likes to make friends with residents; it is said that when you feel a cool breeze by your side, the little boy has taken a liking to you. First-year students report seeing him every year without knowing the legend. He has been known to take students' keys and Rambler cards as well.

Gardiner Hall

Gardiner Hall was dedicated in 1966 and is named after Mabel Gardiner, a former history professor and dean of women. It has the distinction of being one of the most famously haunted residence halls on campus and having one of the most convoluted and confusing ghost stories of Shepherd University. I'm going to try to lead you, the reader, through the origins of and many additions and changes to this legend while doing my best to separate fact from fiction.

According to a 1999 edition of *The Picket*, the Shepherdstown University (then college) newspaper, the genesis of the legend was that Gardiner was haunted by an infamous homecoming queen of years past. According to this version, during homecoming week, the homecoming queen to be (she had already been elected, but the court would not be presented until the homecoming football game) was taking a shower when she slipped, fell and hit her head. Her roommate helped her back to her room, where she slipped into a coma, never to wear the homecoming crown. Notice that in this version, the protagonist has no name. The story goes on to say that each year on homecoming, the portrait of Mabel Gardiner that hangs in the building mysteriously turns right-side up, and the ghost of the tragic student walks across the football field as she would have had she lived to be presented with her crowning glory on that fateful homecoming night long ago. Her ghost, it was said, haunted the halls of Gardiner, where alarm clocks would go off on their own and televisions would turn on and off spontaneously.

In the years since that version of the story was published, the ghost has been given a name: Patricia Loy. Certain students are convinced that they have talked to this spirit through a Ouija board and that she prefers to be called Patty. They also allege that the ghost has told them she is the one who died in the shower by hitting her head and is the one responsible for the supernatural hijinks around the facility. The legend has also expanded to include further details: the portrait of Mabel Henshaw Gardiner must be always turned upside down, and the number of the room in which the spirit supposedly died (which some say is 211 and others say is 311; whichever it is, it's supposed to be on the second floor) must also remain upside down. If the ghost is not appeased with these special accommodations, the students must face the wrath of Patty and whatever retaliation she has up her transparent sleeves. The reasoning behind all these shenanigans has never been clearly explained. Supposedly, Patty blames Mabel Gardiner for her death for some unknown reason—but again, the logic here strains credibility. Mabel Gardiner died in 1952, long before this dormitory ever came to be, so why would this ghost have a grudge against her? Your guess is as good as mine.

What is true from this very tall tale is that there really was a Patricia Loy who attended Shepherd College and lived at Gardiner Hall on the third floor. She was from Romney, West Virginia, and was majoring in education. Patty's life did end tragically, though not in a shower in her dorm. On July 22, 1988, she was killed in a car crash in the early morning hours while driving home to Romney from her job. She was twenty years old. In the Senior Wills section of *The Picket*, she was described by a roommate as someone who loved to frequent Tuesday Night Jams at the Reunion and going on trips to nearby Spook Hill in Maryland. She is buried in Ebenezer Cemetery in Romney.

So who is the real ghost of Gardiner Hall, and how did the tragic death of Patricia Loy evolve into the wildly far-fetched hullabaloo of today? There seems to be no doubt that there really is a ghostly resident kicking up a fuss at Gardiner. Cold spots, disembodied footsteps, toilets flushing and unexplained lights are said to be its handiwork. One witness claimed to have seen her appear in a mirror, with long, brown hair and wearing all white. Perhaps it really is the Patricia Loy who tragically died while she was a student at Shepherd University and she has not been able to let go of the unfinished business she had here, unable to achieve her dream of graduating and embarking on her adult life and career. Who can say—but I highly doubt that she is concerned about portraits and room numbers being turned upside down.

THATCHER HALL

The B Wing of Thatcher Hall is said to be haunted by restless spirits whose graves were disturbed. It's claimed that when construction of the B Wing was taking place, tombstones were moved from an old cemetery adjacent to the building. The only cemetery in the area that I've been able to—possibly—connect to this legend is Rose Hill, an old African American cemetery. Anyone who has ever seen the 1982 movie *Poltergeist* knows what happens whenever headstones in a cemetery are moved when they stand in the way of construction and urban sprawl: the stones get moved, but the bodies remain beneath the earth. While that movie was a very extreme and sensational depiction of the consequences of such actions, the dead do seem to like to make their disapproval known to the living who reside in their desecrated space.

The stereotypical woman in white is said to be one of the apparitions that is seen in the hall of this wing. Years ago, a female student was studying one evening while her roommate was down the hall visiting some friends. She had the radio on for background music when, suddenly, the stations started changing. She got up to fix it, thinking that the station had faded out. When she returned to studying, she felt a chilly breeze in the room. Assuming that the window was open, she turned her head to check the window, and out of the corner of her eye, she saw a picture frame on her shelf fly into the air and crash against the wall, breaking glass everywhere. Completely terrified, the girl ran from the room screaming. When she returned with an RA, the picture frame was back on the shelf and the broken glass was stacked neatly in front of it.

MILLER HALL

Of all the alleged hauntings across the sprawling campus of Shepherd University, the single dormitory that is the most infamous and has the ghostliest activity is none other than Miller Hall. It was the first dormitory built on the west side of campus, in 1915. It was named after Thomas Miller, who was president of the college from 1909 to 1920.

One legend associated with this building says that a girl around the age of twelve with long, dark hair and dressed in Victorian-era fashions haunts this building as well as Turner Hall. She has been seen many times in the

Miller Hall, the most haunted building on the Shepherd University Campus, where an exorcism is alleged to have occurred. *Author's collection.*

rooms and halls of Miller by students and staff. She is said to be linked to the Schley family, who owned the property before Shepherd University acquired the land in 1915. The story goes that the young girl fell from the hayloft of the barn on the property and died. It's quite a sad story, but it is not in the least bit true. The Schley family had no daughter who died, and the property was not a farm; it was just land. The information about the freak accident of the little girl was obtained from students playing with a Ouija board but has been passed off as fact and continues to be repeated. However, the sightings of this mysterious apparition are real. Extensive research has been done to try to uncover the identity of this spirit, but it has ended in puzzling dead ends (no pun intended!). We may never find out her identity, as she seems confused, according to psychics who have connected with her. The story of the Victorian ghost girl is just one of many about Miller Hall.

Another legend says that an unknown nursing student was falling behind in her studies and failing miserably, so she fell into a state of depression and despair. An October 1999 edition of *The Picket* stated that she hanged herself in her room, but the popular, widely told version states that she hanged herself in the attic. Though this story has never been verified, many believe this ghost haunts the dormitory's attic as well as the room in which she resided. According to *The Picket*, if you stand outside the building in just the right place and look up at just the right angle, you can see a light shining brightly in the attic, where the ghost resides. On all occasions, the attic is locked and the stairs are closed off, so there could be no one up there. People would see a figure standing in the window, and there was a figure that would pace the hallways. Some students who managed to gain access to the restricted attic area claimed to have gotten photographs containing strange anomalies. A student who lived in Miller in 1997 reported an incident in which scathing messages were left on all the dry erase boards one evening. They were threats from "the person who lived upstairs." Supposedly, the students were disturbing this person. The strange thing about the messages was that they were on every single door that had a whiteboard, and they were written backward, like looking at the reflection in the mirror of something you've written.

In the 1980s, a Catholic priest reportedly performed an exorcism in room 201 due to residents being ill at ease and feeling a supernatural presence. A student carved a cross into the wood of the door, which has since been replaced. It is likely that, in fact, a blessing was performed; an exorcism would have required permission from the Vatican.

In 2014, several psychics were allowed into Miller Hall while students were not occupying it. Many experienced and saw people from different time periods: men, women, some children, nature spirits and negative entities. One very gifted and talented psychic medium went up to the notorious attic and saw a man and a woman dressed in Civil War–era clothing, but nothing was picked up on the student who committed suicide. When they entered one of the rooms, the psychics immediately felt that rituals had taken place in it. They saw candles all around. Whether it was a séance, something to do with the Ouija board or something else, they couldn't tell. They also felt a negative presence, one that showed itself as a slithery, eel-like entity. The psychics decided to leave the room, and when they did so, the door slammed shut behind them of its own accord. One of them asked the director of the building which room had the cross scratched on the door, and the director told her it was the very room that they were in. If an exorcism or a blessing had taken place there, it didn't work. At that time, students were no longer being assigned to that room, as many who stayed there became depressed, got ill or just dropped out of school—though I'm told that it is now being used again because the school needed the extra space. Another room had salt placed along the inner window ledges in an attempt to keep spiritual forces out of the space—though the person who did this must've been misinformed, because this method of protection uses salt placed on the threshold *outside* of an entranceway or window to keep ethereal intruders out. Placing it inside would keep anything present trapped within.

The building runs the gamut of the paranormal arsenal: everything from whitish mists to strange noises and water faucets turning on by themselves. Photographs of the halls are sometimes marred by white mists superimposed on the environment. Residents experience objects being moved and sightings of a bluish figure sitting in a chair in the dorm. There is also a male figure seen smoking on the upper porch of the building.

Why would so many spirits from so many different eras, seemingly with no direct connection to the building or the land, be in Miller Hall? As stated previously, Miller Hall was not built until 1915, on land that was basically just a lot. Some of the psychics who investigated it felt there was a portal here, an invisible gateway to the spirit realm. One psychic felt that the building was on Native American land. A former resident who used to work at the metaphysical shop in town, On the Wings of Dreams, would frequently have students come into the store who were staying in this dorm, asking how to get rid of "something."

The Yellow House

One of the only surviving structures from the colonial settlement that was to become Shepherdstown is known as the Yellow House. Originally built of logs and now clad in wood siding, it has been owned by Shepherd University since 1926. This quaint little home was converted into a "model home and kitchen" and used for several years to hold courses in home economics. It was built sometime between 1770 and 1793. This historic gem is the setting for one of the oldest legends in the lore of Shepherdstown.

In 1910, the Yellow House was the home of local cobbler (shoemaker) George Yontz and, according to the traditional tale, his furry companion, a cat named Ham. Yontz was very dedicated to his trade; it was said you could hear the *tap*, *tap*, *tap* of him hammering his shoes even late into the night. He was thought to be a rather reclusive, eccentric individual, and it was rumored among the locals that he had amassed a small fortune, which he had hidden on the property. One cold December morning, Yontz's body was found not far from the cabin. Locals assumed he had been killed for his money, though none was ever found when the home was searched.

Ham, the pet cat, was still in the house, and when a Miss Nettie Entler moved in shortly after the cobbler's funeral, she decided to adopt the orphaned feline. On the first anniversary of the cobbler's death, the cat began to act strangely. Early in the morning, he began to prowl restlessly around the small room downstairs, keeping his eyes glued to the attic door. By the time night came, he had begun scratching wildly and fiercely at the attic door. Finally, Miss Entler opened the attic door. From the attic came horrible sounds, like those of a terrific battle. The cat disappeared into the darkness of the attic. Within an hour, the sounds ceased. The cat slipped tiredly down the stairs and dropped silently to the floor. This was repeated every year on the anniversary of Yontz's death until the cat's demise. The yearly battle continued in full force until the house became college property, according to the legend.

Another version of the tale says that a family lived in the cottage with their pet black cat. One night, while the family was gathered around the fireplace, they heard a *tap-tap-tapping* coming from the attic. They realized it was the tapping of a cobbler working on a pair of shoes. The cat headed upstairs to the attic and, moments later, came shrieking down the steps, crashed through the nearest window and disappeared into the night, never to be seen again. The ghostly tapping is said to still tantalize and taunt the ears of those in the vicinity of the haunted little home, especially at the witching hour on Halloween night.

This is a very well-known legend in Shepherdstown; however, as is the case with most legends, research reveals some gaping holes in this story. George Yontz was born in and raised in Shepherdstown and was the son of the late Cornelius Yontz. When the Civil War began, he enlisted in Company B, Second Virginia Regiment, and was faithful in the performance of his duty. When the Second Regiment Band was organized, he was detailed as a musician, and later, when this band was merged into the famous Stonewall Brigade Band, he became a member of that organization. After the war, he worked at his trade, that of a shoemaker, in Shepherdstown, Charles Town and Winchester. While in Winchester, he married, and together, he and his wife had one son. He later came back to Shepherdstown, where he did settle into the little house on High Street, opposite Shepherd College. For reasons unknown, his wife and child did not live with him. He lived alone in the house, continued to work at the shoemaker's trade and did repair work for the townsfolk. In December 1910, customers showed up at the house and could get no response when they called him or knocked on the door, though several said they'd seen him around the place that afternoon.

Yellow House, located on the Shepherd University campus, is home to one of Shepherdstown's oldest legends. *Author's collection.*

The next morning, it was suggested that he might need attention. The police forced their way into the house and went upstairs, where they found Mr. Yontz's body lying on the floor, cold in death; he had evidently been dead for several hours. The death certificate listed his cause of death as heart failure. His relatives were summoned and, later, took the body to the home of his nephew, where it was prepared for burial. He was interred in the soldiers' lot in Elmwood Cemetery.

There was absolutely no mention of murder or even suspected foul play in George Yontz's obituary, so how exactly did the story become sensationalized to include such details? Was it just rumors and gossip from townsfolk who needed a little drama and mystery in their lives? The house is described in old newspaper accounts as being much more secluded on the lonely hill where it is situated, and the street was enshrouded in total darkness with no streetlights. Old photographs of the house do reveal that the house was surrounded by trees and did seem to appear isolated, which probably inspired such tales and its aura of mystery. Today the house seems much less goosebump-inducing due to the changing environment and modern evolution.

As a side note, in recent years, a very reliable psychic claimed she saw a body outside of the house and that a murder over money had taken place. The house is still believed to be spirit occupied, and mists and other strange things have been photographed through the windows. Perhaps someone else lived there over its long history who was murdered, and the stories have gotten mixed up in the retelling over the years.

CHAPTER 19

THE MYSTERY OF FIERY MANSION

SHEPHERDSTOWN, JEFFERSON COUNTY

Just outside the hustle and bustle of Shepherdstown's lively downtown area is a winding country road that takes travelers along the shores of the Potomac River. Though it is not far from the heavily populated streets of the historic hamlet, its desolation and solitude seem far removed from the vibrancy of the thriving small town. The thick woods and the ebb and flow of the Potomac River are quiet and peaceful and yet foreboding. When twilight envelops the area in darkness, the looming trees and dense foliage lend themselves to many wandering thoughts and imaginings of an assortment of specters and cryptids concealed from the eyes of nervous drivers. This road is no stranger to things that go bump in the night. During the horse-and-buggy days, the old-timers claimed that the ghost of a Civil War soldier would haunt you if you didn't close your eyes while passing the old cement plant near the natural caves. Horses would spook unless their heads were covered, or they would refuse to pass the area.

On Trough Road, just off the old River Road, there once was a house with a fearsome reputation. It was a place known to the locals as Fiery Mansion and was the genesis for one of Shepherdstown's scariest legends. The story that has been passed down through generations is that it was once the home of a dentist who had an office in Shepherdstown, known as Dr. Fiery. His wife was paralyzed from the waist down and was confined to a wheelchair. One summer evening, Dr. Fiery went into town to his office and left his wife upstairs in the bedroom, brushing her hair. On returning home, he was horrified to find the lifeless body of his wife lying at the bottom of the staircase with the wheelchair on top of the poor, unfortunate woman. An expression of absolute terror was seemingly frozen on her face, as if she had seen something nightmarish. It is said that her once-dark hair turned ashen white from the indescribable fear that filled her heart in that final moment before her tragic plunge down the stairs. The legend states that whatever she had seen, Dr. Fiery also saw, because he fled the house, never to be seen or heard from again. The only thing he took with him was the clothes on his back. Everything remained in the house, including the food in the fridge and the vehicle in the garage. He mysteriously disappeared without a trace.

As a result of these bizarre circumstances, the house's sinister reputation began to grow, and people became both fearful of and fascinated with the deserted property. Rumors began to circulate that the house was haunted. It became abandoned and derelict as the passage of time unfolded through the years and became a hot spot for thrill-seeking teenagers, who would sneak into the empty, secluded home on dares. Some of these curious trespassers claimed to have had encounters with the supernatural. Stephen Brown recorded the legend of this house in his classic book *Haunted Houses of Harpers Ferry*. According to the author, he interviewed witnesses who recounted their experiences. One person said they went to the house late one night with several friends, and they heard "the loudest bloodcurdling scream" behind them, followed seconds later by another scream heard down the lane. Another man recounted his experience: he went through the empty house exploring without incident, but when he came out of the house and started to get into his car, he heard a rumbling sound, as if the house was caving in. When he looked back, the house was standing intact, almost deceptively silent. It's said there were several witnesses to this event. A man and his wife went to the house one afternoon, intrigued by the stories they had heard. They parked down the lane and were approaching the house when they saw the shadowy figure of a woman in a long white dress standing in the window. The apparition began to fade, disappearing altogether. Another man claimed to have seen a "fearsome figure" that is the agent of all the ghostly happenings and the catalyst for the tragic event that unfolded there. Other stories are told of people stealing dental tools that were left behind from Dr. Fiery's sudden departure. Allegedly, when they returned home with the stolen items, they would disappear, only to reappear in the crumbling old house.

A local woman who is a lifelong resident of Shepherdstown claimed that when she was a child, many years ago, her grandmother and her mother took her to the house. While standing outside, she saw a woman sitting in a chair

The former site of Fiery Mansion. The only thing that remains is the old garage where Dr. Fiery left his car when he allegedly fled the property. *Courtesy of Mary Howell.*

looking down at them from an upstairs window. She asked her grandmother who the woman was, and while her grandmother didn't confirm whether she, too, saw the figure, she began to tell her granddaughter the legend of the house and claimed the woman she saw was the tormented soul of Ms. Fiery, forever trapped at the site of her untimely death.

The woman and her brother told me that their grandparents knew Dr. Fiery and his paraplegic wife. They claimed their grandfather helped the dentist remodel the home before they moved in. As far as the brother recalled, this was sometime in the 1960s, but he couldn't be positive. He and his sister both claimed that the house was white and once had a long porch across the front of it, which was later changed when the house eventually was remodeled, many years later, after sitting abandoned for decades. Though the place became known as Fiery Mansion, he said it was most definitely not a "mansion"; it was a nice home but nothing special. Both he and his sister said their grandparents confirmed some details of the story involving the wife being wheelchair bound and found at the bottom of the stairs and the dentist vanishing and leaving everything behind at the house. Intriguingly, his grandparents said that the police at the time suspected foul play and that Dr. Fiery had murdered his wife, pushing the wheelchair-bound woman down the stairs as a method of instant divorce. They theorized that he then decided to skip town to a destination unknown to begin a new life.

This gentleman told me that his grandparents could not confirm the famous details of the legend involving the woman's hair turning white from fright or the dentist's harrowing escape by foot into the night as if he was Ichabod Crane being pursued by the headless horseman in "The Legend of Sleepy Hollow." The locals seemed to feel that those details were embellishments that were later added.

So the question is: Was the house haunted before the tragic death—and possible homicide—of Dr. Fiery's wife, or did it become haunted as a result of it? Or was it ever haunted at all? For as many people who claim to have encountered weird happenings at the house, there are just as many who claim that nothing strange ever happened to them while they were in the house. The man who recounted his grandparents' memories claimed he himself encountered nothing while inside the notorious house on Halloween night, nor did a man who lived across the street from the house for years. Others who trespassed in the house in pursuit of ghosts also claimed to come away disappointed that they had an uneventful visit. Over the years, some people lived in the house, and as mentioned earlier, some remodeling was done much later to the property, but for whatever reason, the house was torn down some twenty years ago. All that remains is an empty lot with the garage where Dr. Fiery's old car was left all those years ago when the house was mysteriously vacated. The legendary location of the famous old haunted house broods silently, itself seemingly haunted by the ghosts and memories of its past. This is the classic haunted house story, containing all the essential elements: scandal and, possibly, murder; an abandoned old house in a rural, desolate setting; a haunted reputation; teenagers daring each other to enter the house in an adolescent rite of passage of sorts. This was a popular story for decades in the Shepherdstown area, and though the house is long gone, the story of the many unanswered questions and unsolved mysteries attached to the property will continue to be told and will likely remain firmly embedded in Shepherdstown lore to tantalize and weave its eerie spell for future generations to come.

Chapter 20
More Lore from Shepherdstown

Shepherdstown, Jefferson County

When it comes to ghosts, Shepherdstown has no shortage of stories and legends about invisible intruders. Like the best folklore from any historic town, they all have their roots in the rich history of the region.

The entire Eastern Panhandle contains an abundance of Native American history. The Shawnee, Delaware (Lenape), Tuscarora, Catawba and other tribes traveled through this area specifically to hunt and had temporary encampments. In 1754, during the French and Indian War, settlers clashed with Native Americans and were leaving the area until Shepherdstown's founder, Thomas Shepherd, offered them an incentive to stay by providing them with the opportunity of land grants to build homes. Along with their uneasy relationship with the settlers, some of the tribes fought with each other, notably the Catawba and the Delaware. According to an old story, the Catawba buried a noted Delaware chief alive after one of their clashes, at Swearingen's Spring, which is on the Potomac about half a mile above Shepherdstown. The water from this spring is said to jut out in spurts, and this, the Indians declared, was caused by the heartbeats of the imprisoned Indian chief buried at its source. There are some who believe that there are other Native American burial grounds in the area, and some have reported hearing Native drums late in the night in the area outside of town called Falling Springs, which is about a mile from Shepherdstown.

There is another legend associated with the unrest between the Catawba and Delaware tribes. According to this legend, a Delaware brave fell in love

The Rumsey Monument, a memorial to steamboat inventor James Rumsey. Visitors claim to have seen him riding his steamboat up the Potomac River. *Courtesy of the Library of Congress.*

with a Catawba maiden and went south to steal her from her tribe. On their way back north, they missed the trail leading to Packhorse Ford (an area of the Potomac near Washington County, Maryland) and came out on a cliff of rocks overlooking the river. Their pursuers were coming up behind them, and the only thing to do was jump, so he and his sweetheart leaped over the cliff to sudden death. Since that time, the rocks, located at James Rumsey Monument, have borne the name Lover's Leap.

Speaking of the Rumsey Monument, this towering edifice pierces the sky, majestically memorializing James Rumsey, Shepherdstown's famous inventor of the steamboat. According to a legend that is said to have been verified by nighttime visitors to the Rumsey Park, James Rumsey has been seen making his annual midnight voyage in his little steamboat down the Potomac, stopping only for a few brief moments to gaze at his old home place, the Rumsey House.

Yet another spirited tale involves a certain restaurant owner who used to have an apartment located in a building with an enclosed balcony above it on German Street. She often heard noises, footsteps and commotion but assumed it was tenants of the building—until everyone moved out except her, and she still heard the noises. She thought it odd that there were plumbing fixtures in every room and a secret door to other apartments in her closet.

One day, an elderly man was talking to her in her restaurant and asked her where she lived. When she told him, he said when he was a child, his father would frequent that building, and he told her what it used to be. It seems the building was a place of "ill repute," meaning it was used for prostitution in the early twentieth century. Rumor has it that someone hanged themselves in the stairway. Since the time that the business owner lived in the building, other people who have lived there have confirmed that there is a lot of unexplained activity. The businesses on the first floor report no activity, but residents on the second floor report hearing heavy footsteps on the stairs and unexplained noises and smelling tobacco and an odor that's described as "wet leather" or a "moldy tack room." Sometimes people passing by the building beneath the balcony will catch a whiff of the strong aroma of tobacco.

Shepherdstown is a magical place with a unique aura and an energy that is infectious in all the best possible ways. It is a small town with big stories that is loved by both the living and the dead!

CHAPTER 21

THE HAINTS OF HARPER CEMETERY

HARPERS FERRY, WEST VIRGINIA

The center of tourism in the Eastern Panhandle as well as one of the top tourist destinations in the state is Harpers Ferry National Historic Park. Renowned for its panoramic views of the surrounding mountain vistas, it's steeped in both pivotal American history and folklore and legendary tales of spooks and spirit-infested buildings.

One of the most stunning views in the park can be found high atop the mountain, above St. Peter's Catholic Church and the famed Jefferson Rock. Harper Cemetery spreads over a sprawling hill carpeted by lush lawns and weatherworn tombstones. On a clear day, the cotton-like clouds punctuating the blue sky seem to be within human reach from the dizzying heights of the cemetery. This peaceful, tranquil setting is like a microcosm of Harpers Ferry history. One notable burial is that of the founder of the town, Robert Harper. Hailing from Pennsylvania, an architect by trade, he was immediately taken with the breathtaking beauty and commerce potential of the waterpower offered by the Potomac and Shenandoah Rivers. He had been contracted to build a Quaker church in the Shenandoah Valley, and as fate would have it, he passed through this picturesque valley. The enchantment of the unique setting immediately cast its spell on him, and he decided to settle there permanently.

At the time of his death in 1782, there were only houses in the tiny little town. Harper had foreseen the potential growth and expansion of the community and set aside this four-acre cemetery. Harper's grave is surrounded by many markers of Irish and German immigrants who settled

Jefferson Rock. Its high vantage point offers stunning views of Harpers Ferry. *Courtesy of the Library of Congress.*

in the area in the 1830s, as well as many other notable citizens who played a part in Harpers Ferry's rich narrative.

The cemetery is a lovely sanctuary for reflection and solitude, far removed from the busy sidewalks of the town below, which are packed full of eager tourists from all over the world. As is to be expected, however, darkness brings out an assortment of restless spirits eternally wandering among the endless array of tombstones.

One of the most memorable and eccentric of Harpers Ferry's past residents was a character known as Dr. Brown. He is said to have been a native of Scotland and served as a surgeon for the American army during the Revolution. He cared for Indians and was a member of the United States cavalry. The War Department stationed him in the Ferry to attend to the needs of the workers at the armory. He drew a pension from the government in addition to the income from his medical career. A man of financial substance, he indulged his odd eccentricities at his bachelor cabin on High Street. A partially natural, partially man-made cave near his residence was used as his storehouse and a dispensary. He had a tremendous love of dogs and cats, and no fewer than fifty dogs would be seen following him about town. The howls in the night became a nuisance in the sleepy little village. Cruel young men of the place would wait until the doctor was out of town

Harper Cemetery contains many graves of the early settlers of Harpers Ferry, dotting the hillside. *Author's collection.*

and would shoot many of the poor canines. Despite his odd nature, he was known for being a generous-hearted soul who never charged the armory workers for medical advice.

Dr. Brown died around the year 1824, and on his deathbed, he made a very strange request. He ordered that his coffin should be made with a glass window in the lid and that he should be placed in a standing position in a brick vault he had constructed in the cemetery. His odd instructions further stated that his coffin should be left in that position for nine days after his burial, at which point his corpse would reanimate and he would rise from the dead. A person was employed to visit the vault every day until the promised resurrection, when they were to help him from his custom-made coffin housed within the brick vault. This miraculous event never took place: Dr. Brown's body was as cold and lifeless as the neighboring bodies buried beneath the earth. A proper, conventional burial never took place, and the vault began to erode and crumble into pieces with the passage of time. The skull separated from the body and lay exposed on the hillside near the vault for years. Children returning home from school taking shortcuts through the cemetery began playing games of kickball with the skull—certainly not the outcome poor Dr. Brown had predicted.

One hundred years later, a gentleman from Pennsylvania wrote a letter to the superintendent of the John Brown Farm in North Elba, New York. In that letter, he claimed to have the skull of John Brown, the abolitionist. After much debate, it was decided that this was impossible, because John Brown's grave had not been disturbed. Nevertheless, the skull in question was sent to North Elba and now lies buried in the same spot as the famous John Brown, the raider. Could it be that Dr. Brown's skull occupies the grave alongside old John Brown's rotting bones?

Dr. Brown's cabin was destroyed during the Civil War, but the enlarged natural cave that housed his medicines can still be seen today from Potomac Street. On nights when the moon illuminates the sky above the old cemetery and elongated shadows from the tombstones stretch over the hillside, the headless figure of a man is seen roaming the grounds. He is said to be Dr. Brown, still searching for his lost head. Perhaps he really did return from the dead—only in spirit, not in the flesh.

There is a gnarly, ancient tree located in the middle of the cemetery that has an old, forgotten legend attached to it. It's said that there were two young lovers in town who came from very different backgrounds. The girl came from a family of "gypsies" and fell in love with a young man outside of her community. Her family fiercely objected to the relationship, but the two were in love and wanted to consummate their commitment in marriage. The girl's angry family decided to punish her for her disobedience and placed a curse on the innocent young lovers: if they couldn't keep them apart in life, they would be separated in death. It is said that after the deaths of the loving married couple, they were buried side by side in Harper Cemetery.

Harper Cemetery offers stunning views of the surrounding countryside. *Author's collection.*

Shortly after, a tree began growing between the two graves. The tree became larger, extending its branches, and the widening trunk pushed the graves farther apart. Attempts were made to cut down the tree, but it continued to spring back to life in its mission to fulfil its purpose. Some say you can still see evidence of the many attempts to stop the ever eager tree in the indentations and gashes found in the scarred trunk. If you visit, look for an old tree situated in about the middle of the cemetery. You will see two ancient tombstones leaning to each side of its trunk: two doomed lovers forever separated in death by a vengeful curse.

The allegedly cursed tree in Harper Cemetery. *Author's collection.*

One of the eeriest tales told of this historic burial ground concerns a young woman named Pam who was walking through the cemetery with four of her teenaged friends. It was after midnight on a summer night as they strolled through the thick blackness of the land of the dead. Their visit was abruptly interrupted by a woman wearing a long, flowing dress who came rushing toward them from the dark abyss. The figure screamed, "Give me back my baby!" All five of the terrified teens ran as fast as they could out of the cemetery and down the steep stone steps of the Appalachian Trail, past Jefferson Rock. This is no easy task in full daylight, but in the impenetrable dark of the night, only sheer adrenaline could guide someone down this steep, treacherous mountain. By the time the group reached the church, the raging wraith had ended her pursuit of them and vanished from sight. A local told me that this frightening yet pathetic spirit is a permanent fixture of the cemetery and regularly makes appearances.

Who this woman is and what happened to her baby is unknown, but perhaps they were victims of the devastating 1850 outbreak of Asiatic cholera, an intestinal disease caused by water contaminated with fecal matter. It visited the homes of both rich and poor and showed no discrimination in the victims it chose. Over one hundred people in the village perished during the epidemic, and all who could leave fled, leaving the town deserted and businesses paralyzed. Perhaps the woman and her infant were among the unfortunate victims, and she still has not accepted the cruel hand that fate dealt her, desperately seeking to be reunited with her child.

One of the most visually arresting and beloved monuments in the cemetery is a grave site adorned with a stone angel. It's a fitting tribute for the grave of Montana Eleanor Gannon, who was weeks away from her fourth birthday when she passed away on June 25, 1893. She was the only child of Dr. William Henry Gannon, a physician in Harpers Ferry, and his wife, Mary Gannon.

An interesting bit of history concerning this statue is that until 2016, the angel's left wing tip had been missing since the 1970s. In the 1960s, an architect worked on several historic sites in the town. He and his wife loved the area and even wed at St. Peter's Catholic Church. During a return trip to town in the 1970s, they visited the cemetery and made a stop at Montana Gannon's grave. The architect had always admired the stone angel and had visited it often while working there. They found a broken stone wing tip on the ground near the grave and picked it up, intending to contact the National Park Service to determine how best to replace it on the statue. The busy couple didn't contact NPS officials right away, and then they moved

Left: Statue of Montana Eleanor Gannon. For many years, one wing tip was missing, but it was eventually restored. *Author's collection.*

Opposite: The rolling hill that Harper Cemetery is situated on is said to be a place where strange things happen at twilight. *Author's collection.*

into a new home. The wing, safely wrapped in a box, went too but got stashed away, forgotten in the attic. After the architect's death in 2011, his wife began sorting through their belongings and came across the forgotten wing tip. She contacted the National Park Service, and eventually the wing tip was reattached to its rightful place, making the cherished statue whole once again.

Not much is known about the very short life of little Montana other than that she died in Manhattan, New York. Her cause of death is unknown, but what a bitter pill it must have been to swallow for her father, who was a doctor—dedicated to the health and well-being of others yet unable to save the life of his own child. He was only forty-seven years of age when he died, only a few years later, in Brunswick, Maryland. After her husband's death, Mary Gannon moved to Boise, Idaho, and worked as a teacher until her death in 1935.

Some claim that the spirit of young Montana Eleanor Gannon still wanders the beautiful yet lonely site of her final resting place. The apparition of a female child has been seen near the angelic sculpture.

Many have reported strange encounters on this hallowed hill. A lady walking though the cemetery was startled by a strange phenomenon involving a flowing mist emanating from behind a singular tombstone while the rest of the cemetery was fog-free. Another young man was on his way to meet some friends down at the Catholic church; while he was trekking through the labyrinth of stones, an unseen force grabbed him from behind and spun him around. He completed the rest of the journey to meet up with his friends in record time.

Others tell stories of seeing groups of Civil War soldiers walking through the cemetery. Undoubtedly, the location's high vantage point was of strategic use to them during the war, and some of them are interred for eternity beneath the soil of the cemetery. Some claim to have seen glowing spheres of light navigating the landscape, glowing tombstones and even wispy white forms seemingly dancing in the moonlight. As one resident once described it to me, "It is both a fun and scary place to visit."

CHAPTER 22

THE RESTLESS REVENANT

HARPERS FERRY, JEFFERSON COUNTY

The ghosts of Harpers Ferry are plentiful, and they have been thoroughly documented in many other collections of West Virginia ghost stories and further preserved through the long-running ghost tours of the historic park. The mission of this book is to share some of the lesser-known, more obscure tales of the region, and for that reason, many of the more easily accessible and popular stories are not included in this publication. One story from Harpers Ferry that's not really divulged in any form these days is, in this writer's opinion, one of the eeriest and most memorable legends from this beloved town. It was immortalized by the iconic Shirley Dougherty on her memorable ghost tours.

There is a certain redbrick building on the lower end of High Street, just a few stores down from Hog Alley. Many years ago, a couple moved into this dwelling to make a home, in hopes of sharing many happy years together within the ancient walls of the structure. Some of the locals warned the couple prior to their purchase of the property that it was haunted, but they chose to ignore their warnings as fanciful campfire fodder from superstitious townsfolk.

One afternoon, they came home to find that their cherished piece of Aztec pottery—a little man with an impressive headdress and folded arms—had been removed from its shelf in the living room and shattered to pieces on the floor. In one corner of the room was the head; the rest of the statue was found strewn around the carpeted room. The pieces were carefully glued together, and the statue was returned to its rightful place on the shelf. One week later, the poor harassed statue was once again found across the room, only decapitated this time He was accompanied by some small books and a framed picture with the glass cracked that had shared the shelf with the statue. Once again, the statue was pieced back together and returned to the shelf, only to meet the same fate for a third time—after which the decision was promptly made to relocate it to a different spot in the room.

The couple began to hear knocks on the walls and a strange ticking sound that would suddenly extinguish itself. After four nights of being disturbed by the curious noises, they were jolted awake by a thunderous banging on the plaster walls at a tremendous volume, quickly followed by the slow, steady ticking noise. A few weeks later, while they were in their living room, they heard the back door creaking open downstairs. On investigation, the door was found standing wide open; they promptly secured it with a bolt and chain. This happened a second time; only this time, they knew the door had been closed and properly secured and there was no negligence on their part.

On another afternoon, the couple came home to find a pair of pewter candlesticks, made by the town pewter smith, on the floor, bent and twisted, with the clear indention of fingers left behind in the hard metal by powerful hands. An even more nerve-jangling event transpired on another return home, when they found an elaborate and intricately carved letter *J* etched into a rippled old windowpane. It was both astounding and impressive in its otherworldly craftsmanship.

The disturbances within the home continued with unrelenting stamina. Paintings fell to the floor with their cords unbroken and the nails in place and intact. Food would be found yanked from the kitchen cupboards and spilled onto the floor. The walls continued to reverberate with the persistent knocking. The house seemed to be possessed by a force that was determined to make its presence known to the frightened residents. The pieces of the puzzle were about to come together in this paranormal nightmare.

One day, a neighbor told them that her great-grandmother, who lived next to their house in 1863, had been an eyewitness to a tragic event that was the key to the mystery of the house. During the Civil War, the house was used as a prison by Union soldiers. The incarcerated Confederates were kept on the top floor, and the guards were housed two floors below. The couple had always been curious about why there were strange writings on the worn plaster walls of the home. They now understood that they were done by the prisoners who had been held captive there long ago.

There was a certain guard named Jacob who met a young lady in town. Like most young, virile males would have been, he was eager to begin a courtship with the buxom lass. They arranged a rendezvous one night, and Jacob talked his comrades into covering for him while he left his post to meet his date. He and his fellow guards had not anticipated a surprise inspection that night. When questioned about why Jacob's post was vacant, the other soldiers tried their best to excuse his absence, but the truth was learned. No good deed goes unpunished, as the old saying goes, and that is exactly what happened to Jacob's coworkers. The resentful young men decided to teach the smitten Jacob a lesson for getting them into trouble for his little dalliance. When he returned, they jumped him, pulling his struggling body to the floor, where they tied his hands and feet. They stuffed feathers in his nose, ears and mouth and poked and punched him for what they thought was a suitable duration of discomfort. After the deed was done, they stood back, away from the battered Jacob, and waited for him to rise from the floor. However, his body was motionless, and they quickly discovered that Jacob would never stand on his feet to resume his duties because he was dead.

This sudden turn of events left the soldiers in a fearful panic. Murder was not their intention; they only wanted to teach him a lesson. What were they to do? They hastily decided to build a makeshift coffin that the body could be stuffed into and discreetly bury him in the backyard under the cover of darkness. When he was discovered missing, the officers would think he had deserted. While transporting the crude box containing the lifeless body of Jacob down the back stairs to the yard, one of the soldiers lost his footing and slipped on the stairs. The casket slid down the stairs and split open, revealing its contents.

The neighbors, awakened by the commotion, immediately ran to their windows to see the soldiers frantically scrambling about to collect the boards from the fractured coffin and remove the spilled corpse. The authorities were notified, and the soldiers were arrested. Jacob is said to have been buried nearby, but the exact location is unknown; presumably it was at Harper Cemetery. Old-timers claimed that the grave site was a plain pauper's grave but that at certain times of the year, the ground above the grave turned scarlet and became strangely damp. Apparitions and peculiar flickering lights are also said to have been seen at the forlorn grave of the unfortunate soldier. Others who lived in the home over the years also bore witness to supernatural manifestations and vacated the home shortly thereafter. Whether poor Jacob ever found peace or the building is still besieged by his tormented soul and the memory of his gruesome demise is unknown. Perhaps those who occupy the space prefer not to say or deal with the disturbances privately.

According to Shirley Dougherty's book *A Ghostly Tour of Harpers Ferry*, there is another spine-chilling twist to this building's troubled past. During World War I, soldiers were sent to Harpers Ferry to guard the railroad. They camped by the river, but high water forced them to move into town. Jacob's house on High Street was vacant, so some of them were housed there. Soon the townspeople noticed that there was one soldier who seemed to be the object of bullying and ridicule. They witnessed many cruel tricks being played on the poor lad. One day, they found him standing on a tree stump with a noose around his neck. The antagonizing soldiers were urging him to jump. A few days later, the poor abused soldier was found in his bed with his hands and his feet bound and his mouth and nose stuffed with cotton. Was it just an eerie coincidence that during two wars, two murders were committed in the same manner in this building?

CHAPTER 23
ANGEL OF DEATH

HARPERS FERRY, JEFFERSON COUNTY

The alternately peaceful and turbulent waters that surround the quaint little hamlet of Harpers Ferry are a confluence of two rivers, the Shenandoah and the Potomac. Shirley Dougherty chronicled an old Indian origin story in her book *A Ghostly Tour of Harpers Ferry*. According to her rendition of the old folktale, Shenandoah was an Indian chief's daughter. She passed through this area with her tribe while they were searching for new hunting grounds. They did not expect to meet up with an enemy tribe, but being warriors, they were not about to back down from opposition and wholeheartedly engaged in a fierce battle. Soon after, Shenandoah met up with a brave from the enemy tribe named Potomac. They soon became star-crossed lovers. Shenandoah's father was outraged at his daughter's fraternization with the enemy and forbid the relationship. He sent his daughter away, separating her from her beloved Potomac. His devastated daughter escaped to the mountains of the Great Blue Ridge, and the secluded wilderness became a refuge for her broken spirit. It is said that the young woman grieved and grieved until her already broken heart finally ceased to beat. The endless tears she shed formed the Shenandoah River.

When Shenandoah's lost love, Potomac, learned what had happened to his beloved, he fled to the mountains to the west. The fallen tears of his endless sobbing formed the Potomac River. Shenandoah and Potomac are forever joined in Harpers Ferry, where their doomed love affair commenced.

The point where these two rivers meet is very dangerous, and the raging waters have claimed many lives over the years. The deceptively peaceful

The raging waters of the Potomac and Shenandoah Rivers have claimed the lives of many poor unfortunate souls. *Courtesy of the Library of Congress.*

waters can quickly become a raging torrent that can engulf even the most experienced swimmer or fisherman and send them to a watery grave.

Many years ago, nine people drowned in a six-week period during one tragic summer season. However, each death was punctuated by a very odd

occurrence. Each one of the terrible drownings was reported by an elderly man wearing a red plaid shirt and an old pair of baggy trousers. He would be seen rushing from the water's edge and frantically informing the nearest person that someone in the river needed help. When this continued to happen with every drowning that occurred during that span of weeks, the townspeople began to wonder why it always seemed to be this same man, every single time, who was the first to give the alarm.

One of the eyewitnesses to the strange messenger was a young man. One evening, he and his girlfriend went to visit her grandparents. The grandparents shared some old photographs and picture albums of days gone by in Harpers Ferry with their granddaughter's suitor. One of the pictures caught the young man's eye. He recognized a face as being that of the enigmatic character. He learned that the man in the pictures was named Mosa Kline. He had been a peddler in the early 1900s. One fateful night, he started to cross the bridge into Maryland, but he never completed his journey to the other side. Two weeks later, a body was discovered down the river. It was that of the old man. Questions surrounding his untimely death remain unanswered. Did he accidentally fall from the bridge in the dark of the night? Or was he an unfortunate victim of foul play and his body was tossed into the river? We will never know, but for those who encountered Mosa and his urgent pleas for help that tragic summer long ago, there was no doubt that his spirit had returned, desperately seeking help for those drowning in the river, trying to prevent what happened to him from happening to someone else.

CHAPTER 24

THE HOLY GHOSTS OF ST. PETER'S CATHOLIC CHURCH

HARPERS FERRY, JEFFERSON COUNTY

One of the most iconic structures in Harpers Ferry National Park is the majestic edifice of St. Peter's Catholic Church. It towers high above the town, commanding attention both near and far. With its neo-Gothic architecture and Tiffany stained glass windows, its sprawling piazza gives one spectacular views from the heights of its location.

The church was built in the early 1830s on land donated by Robert Harper. It was restored and enlarged in 1889. The church is still fully operational today, and services continue to be held within the gorgeous sanctuary with its marvelous carved Carrara marble altar. The visual beauty and grandeur of this historic structure conceals a turbulent and tumultuous history. St. Peter's was the only church in Harpers Ferry to survive the Civil War intact. It's a proud testament to the resilience of the town and its people during the smoldering violence of the Civil War. The steep, uneven stone steps that lead up to the church, when viewed from the bottom, almost seem like a stairway to the heavens. It is said that those very steps ran red with the blood of the wounded as they were carried up to the church when it was used as a hospital.

One story about the church concerns one of the wounded soldiers who was carried into the church when it was being used as a hospital. The many soldiers needing care were laid out in the piazza and then triaged by those providing medical aid to the injured. This soldier's wounds were not as severe as some of the other soldiers' who were bleeding out around him, so

St. Peter's Catholic Church. One of Harpers Ferry's most recognizable landmarks, it towers over the town, high atop a set of steep stone steps. *Author's collection.*

he was left on the piazza while the others were urgently attended to within the sanctuary. As the evening wore on, the soldier felt himself becoming weaker and weaker, and his wounds and his life began to seep away. Even as consciousness was beginning to fade, he still had faith that help would soon arrive and he would be saved. Finally, his turn arrived, and his bleeding body was removed to a stretcher. As the grateful soldier was carried across the threshold of the church, he was heard to whisper in a labored voice, "Thank God, I'm saved." However, help came too late, and he became yet another tragic casualty among those who were brought to the church for aid but didn't survive. The moment of this young man's passing is believed to have left a profound spiritual imprint on the exterior of St. Peter's. People say that on misty nights, they see a glowing golden mass on the threshold of the church. The disembodied, frail voice of a man can be heard whispering, "Thank God, I'm saved." Others claim to have seen the lifeless body of the fallen soldier lying within the church.

During the Civil War, Father Costello was the dedicated, faithful priest of St. Peter's. He remained behind to attend to his church and employed a most clever strategy that most certainly aided in the structure's survival. Whenever the town was being shelled from Maryland Heights, he would raise a British flag from the steeple. Both sides, fearing an international incident with England, would fire on another target. Father Costello himself helped care for the wounded when the church was a field hospital. One night, it is said, he ventured out, hoping to be concealed by the dark of the night, to tend to some of the wounded soldiers in the town. As he was ascending the stone stairs to return to his church, he was spotted by some of the gunners on Maryland Heights. They opened fire on him, and he managed to dodge the flying bullets and hid until the clouds covered the moon and he could safely resume the climb up the seemingly endless staircase to his destination. Father Costello's dedication and loyalty are legendary, and it's certainly not surprising that it is believed he still returns to watch over his beloved church.

Around six o'clock in the evening, visitors will be passing by the church on their way to Jefferson Rock to take in the breathtaking evening views that it offers of the surrounding countryside. As they pass by the side of the church, they see an elderly priest coming from the rectory wearing a black friar's hat. He's such a quaint little man they that stop to speak with him, but he never acknowledges or returns their greeting. He simply walks past them and then turns and walks right through the doorless wall into the church. His seeming aloofness and obliviousness to the presence of those who encounter him suddenly makes shattering sense. He is not of this world. It is believed that the ghostly priest is passing through a door that once existed in the side wall of the church before the renovations. But as long as his spirit is seen, St. Peter's is in good hands, still being watched over by the ever resourceful and fiercely dedicated Father Costello.

CHAPTER 25

ADAM LIVINGSTON, I PRESUME?

MIDDLEWAY, JEFFERSON COUNTY

Of all the many towns, cities and landmarks that dot the landscape of the Eastern Panhandle, there is one location that commands attention and demands further exploration. The historic village of Middleway is nestled into a sequestered, rural niche of Jefferson County, surrounded by rolling hills, lush pastures and farmland. If there is such a thing as a place having a pulse of its own, this charming, quaint little oasis reverberates with the heartbeat of the past. Seemingly untouched by the urban sprawl that has affected many such locations, it is firmly set in its own time capsule, with all the charm and gentility of a gentrified Mayberry-type environment. This sleepy little village exudes history from every eighteenth- and nineteenth-century structure encompassed by the historic district.

Middleway is located at the intersection of two trails used by Native Americans. When John Smith explored the area in 1729, he found the transportation opportunities of the trails advantageous and discovered the natural water source for the area known as Turkey Run. By 1734, he and his son, along with John's brother Rees, had established grist and hemp mills along Turkey Run. A small farming and milling community had developed by the time the American Revolution commenced. In 1795, the Smith family began selling town lots, and by 1798, the town of Smithfield had been incorporated.

In 1807, a post office was established under the name of Middleway to avoid confusion with the other Smithfield in Tidewater, Virginia. In the 1800s,

Wizard Clip plaque. The village of Middleway commemorated its famous legend by placing markers on the historic homes and buildings adorned with scissors, wizard hats and crescent moons. *Courtesy of the Library of Congress.*

the town was a prosperous trading center with a vibrant and bustling main street. Shops and houses lined the street, and the village boasted two churches as well as three stores, an apothecary, a distillery, four shoemakers, five weavers, one wagonmaker, one saddletree maker, one hatter, three blacksmiths, three tailors and one tanner. An attorney at law and a physician rounded out the business roster of the thriving little hamlet.

After the Civil War and through the 1880s, the town fell on hard times. Many of the town's younger residents left the village for better prospects elsewhere. Even though the once thriving little village had begun a steady decline, the many richly historic buildings remained as a proud testament to the past, and Middleway still retains its status as a small country village where visitors can escape the ever-changing hustle and bustle of the commerce-heavy world and step back in time to a simpler, more peaceful way of life.

One thing that visitors to this historic landmark village immediately notice and are subsequently intrigued by are the plaques marking the ancient structures that are adorned with crescent moons, wizard hats and scissors. These wonderfully quirky signs pay homage to Middleway's main claim to fame, the legend of the Wizard Clip. Yep, this scenic and bucolic little gem was at the center of one of West Virginia's most famous and most documented ghost stories. The tale has been told time and again, is very popular and well known to locals and beyond and has been the subject of entire volumes. For a very thorough, extremely well-researched exploration of every aspect of the legend, I highly recommend the book *The Appalachian Legend of the Wizard Clip* by Michael Kishbucher. The purpose of this book is to highlight the lesser-known tales of the region, so I don't want to go too much in depth with this story when it has already been so thoroughly documented. For the purposes of this book, I will briefly recount the popular legend that is so firmly embedded in the local folklore.

In 1790, Adam Livingston, a Lutheran, moved with his family from Pennsylvania to a farm northwest of present-day Middleway. Prior to

1794, the farm and homestead were seized with inexplicable calamities and otherworldly mayhem. Unusual noises and voices plagued the family, crockery was hurled to the floor and rocks rolled across rooms unassisted by human hands. There was the persistent clipping sound, and clothes were mysteriously cut to pieces, revealing crescent moon shapes. Livestock on the farm were allegedly beheaded by an invisible blade, and the family endured constant spectral torment. People came from far and wide to witness for themselves the seemingly bewitched farm and the supernatural deviltry at play. After several years of these debilitating disturbances, Adam Livingston sought help from several Protestant ministers, who were powerless to stop the spectral onslaught. One night, Adam had a dream in which he saw a figure in a church dressed in black robes, whom he later identified as a Roman Catholic priest he had seen in Shepherdstown. In 1797, Father Cahill and Father Galitzin made several visits to the property, saying prayers and masses and eventually being credited with successfully exorcising the diabolical tormentor. In gratitude for their services, Adam Livingston later converted to Catholicism and donated about thirty-five acres of his farm to the Church, which is now a Catholic pastoral center known as Priest Field.

This is a very simplified recap of events. There is much more detail and depth as well as many facets to this story, which is endlessly fascinating. As a native of the neighboring county, I grew up hearing and reading about the famous Wizard Clip and often wondered if this was the only brush with the supernatural that Middleway had ever had—or were there other ghost stories that were overshadowed by this imposing paranormal epic? As it turns out, Middleway is home to many a haunted tale, which I was delighted to learn about, and I am thrilled to be able to share these tales with you, the reader. Hopefully, you will be as intrigued as I was when I heard them.

The source for these stories is Middleway Conservancy Association president and historian Jessie Norris. She is the creator of and tour guide for the Middleway Ghost Tours and is a huge supporter of the promotion of the village's history and legends.

The firstly ghostly tale that I will recount has its roots in the Civil War, the catalyst for many of the region's spooky tales. Like much of the surrounding countryside, Middleway suffered during the War Between the States. Since Middleway was at the intersection of two important roads and was well equipped with anything a traveler might need, it became a major stopping point for both Union and Confederate soldiers. Several skirmishes occurred in and around the village; the largest engagement was the Battle of Smithfield in August 1864. Union losses were thirty-five killed

Masonic Hall, one of the many historic structures that make up the historic district of Middleway. *Courtesy of the Library of Congress.*

or wounded and Confederate losses ten killed and seventy-five wounded. Several casualties from North Carolina were buried behind the Masonic Hall. One building, which still stands and is undergoing renovations as of this writing, was used as a hospital. At the time of the war, it was where one of the town's four physicians practiced. After the Battle of Antietam, wagons brought wounded soldiers into the town and the building was converted into a makeshift hospital. Due to the amount of bloodshed from the amputated limbs, holes had to be cut out of the floor on the main level and upstairs and pans placed to catch the copious amounts of flowing blood. Mass graves containing the bones from the amputated limbs are said to be located in Middleway, likely near the old former hospital.

One local resident's family has lived in Middleway for well over one hundred years. Years ago, when the man was in his twenties, he was walking past Grace Episcopal Church and graveyard on his way home one night. He noticed two strange men walking around the corner of the Masonic hall and out into the road behind him. He could hear them talking among themselves. Since there were two of them and he was walking alone at night on this quiet, deserted road, he kept a close eye on the men. He turned the corner and then noticed that they had done the same and were quickly approaching him. Much to his surprise, he noticed that they were wearing Confederate soldiers' uniforms. The alarming reality that he had been thrust into a *Twilight Zone* episode of his own became all too apparent. He finally stopped and confronted the two men, questioning them about why they seemed to be shadowing him. The men responded by asking, "Where is the inn? How is the ale there?" Confused and a bit chilled by this seemingly surreal encounter, he responded, "You'll have to check it out for yourselves." The men thanked him and turned and walked through the fence that had replaced the original main gate to get into the back entrance of the Virginia Inn, which was a tavern and one of the main establishments in the town during the Civil War. The shocked young man walked over to the fence where the two soldiers had vanished—and as in any good ghost story, there was nothing there. Others claim to have seen the two soldiers wandering down the road. An eerie twist to this tale is that buried in front of Grace Episcopal Church are the remains of two unknown Confederate soldiers. The pastor of the church says that sometimes, while sitting on the porch

The churchyard of Grace Episcopal contains many graves of the early inhabitants of Middleway. *Author's collection.*

Grace Episcopal Church. There is said to be a shell from a Civil War skirmish embedded in the vestry room door. *Author's collection.*

of the parish rectory in the evening hours, he and his wife will smell the strong scent of tobacco and see a formless shape move quickly through the cemetery. In the blink of an eye, it is gone.

The Virginia Inn's oldest portion is the back section on the Grace Street side. It was built by John Smith around 1750. The front part of the house was used as an inn during the early nineteenth century. The original owner of the house owned slaves, as did most of the property owners in the town. One slave was known as Aunt Suky. She was well known and respected by the residents of the town and endeared herself to all who knew her. Aunt Suky had a daughter who was around twelve years old named Daphne. However, Daphne was one servant too many for the family. Giving the young girl her freedom would result in her having no place to go. Selling her in the community was not an option either, because it could lead to domestic problems for the master. Separating Aunt Suky from her daughter could lead to hostility and animosity from the community and from his family due to the townspeople's respect and admiration of Suky.

The owner decided to meet up with a slave dealer who came through town, and a secret deal was struck as a solution to the dilemma. He gave the dealer a description of Daphne, and the details of this shady transaction were worked out with the utmost secrecy. The plan was kept in strict confidence, and he dared not share a single detail with anyone. The day of the sale arrived, and the oblivious young girl was instructed to walk outside to the water pump with a basket on her arm and wait. The agent had been told to look for the girl carrying the identifying basket at this designated spot. Just as planned, the dealer came along and whisked the poor girl off along with his other purchases far into the South, unbeknownst to anyone.

Aunt Sukie did eventually learn the fate of her beloved daughter, and in her devastation, she vowed that she would never look her master in the eye again. She managed to devise a way to "banish" him from her sight. She fashioned a "slab bonnet" with a large bill that protruded far from the front of it, effectively concealing her face, much like a mourning veil would. She kept her promise to never set eyes on her master's face for his betrayal and wore the hat daily for many years. She always made sure she wore it when her master had guests and family over to ensure it brought embarrassment and discomfort to him.

Residents of Middleway have reported seeing the figure of an African American woman, all dressed in black, donning a bonnet with a very elongated bill obscuring much of her face. Her head is always facing down, and she paces around the front of the old Virginia Inn or sits on a bench or a chair that doesn't exist in the material realm. Folks have claimed to have seen her roaming among other areas of the village as well, still mourning her cruel separation from her daughter at the hands of a devious master.

Scollay Hall is an interesting house that was built in three stages during the eighteenth and early nineteenth centuries. The oldest section predates the Revolutionary War. The main brick section was built by Dr. Samuel Scollay around 1823. In the early 1790s, it was used for Lutheran services conducted by Nicholas Schall. It was also a tavern, a home and a rental at one time.

One renter recalled experiences involving marbles that would roll across the floor in her direction as if enticing her to engage in a game involving unseen participants. In one room of the house, she would sit and read and would hear children giggling and marbles rolling across the floor and into another room. Rather than feeling fearful of these inexplicable encounters, she felt annoyed by her reading being interrupted and would tell the ghostly children to stop and go to bed. Often, the reprimand would work, and her reading would continue uninterrupted. She had been told by the previous owner of the house to be nice to the children, indicating that the activity has been occurring within the building for quite some time.

Ramsey's Tavern is a clapboard log home, probably dating from the late eighteenth century. It is believed to have been used as an inn and tavern in the nineteenth century. It was occupied by Dr. Alan Davis. The house has been restored; additions included a beautiful cathedral kitchen. A previous owner of the house used to find her cake flour open and a trail of flour extending through the house to the staircase. Smudges and floury handprints would be found on the railing of the staircase. On one occasion, she was walking past the kitchen window outside and noticed someone standing in the window, staring out at her. Whenever the flour was discovered, the smell of sweet corn or perhaps cornbread was very prevalent.

The Benjamin Bell House is another small clapboard log home, built in 1810. The previous and current owners have both reported paranormal happenings. The previous owner stated that due to the age of the home and its poor insulation, she would keep the kitchen cabinets open during the winter so the pipes would not freeze. Often, she would walk in to find the cabinet doors closed and would hear them closing while she was in other parts of the house. Once, she walked in, saw one of the cabinets physically closing and heard someone running out of the room snickering like a mischievous child. After about four or five incidents, she finally went into total mom mode and scolded the pranksters, stating, "That's enough! You're not going to close these cabinets anymore. You need to find something else to play with!" The doors stopped closing. On another occasion, the owner was bending down and looking in a cabinet and picked up an item and checked the expiration date. When she discovered that the item was expired, she heard a voice say, "Honey, you don't want to eat that." The woman replied, "Well, I was planning on throwing it away!" At that moment, she felt a cool breeze move past her, and the voice responded, "That's good."

During renovations of the kitchen, the current owners pulled up the floorboards and discovered several small pairs of leather baby shoes from the colonial period that had been placed in the small crawlspace below. Many of the early inhabitants of the village were of German and Irish descent, and there was a tradition of doing such a thing for luck, to ward off evil spirits or when children left home, to ensure that they would never move far away. Current residents of the town who are of German and Irish descent urged the owners to return the items and keep them in their space, because removing them could have consequences that would creep them out far more than the shoes did.

Many of Middleway's unseen residents appear to be engaged in their normal, everyday duties as if they're still living out their lives. There's never an ill feeling or a threatening menace that's reported. But what about Middleway's original spectral hell-raiser? There are those currently living in Middleway who still claim they will occasionally find cloth items or clothing clipped up with the infamous crescent moons. Odd happenings persist at Priest Field and, apparently, still bring some uneasiness to some. According to the book *The Appalachian Legend of the Wizard Clip*, a local priest described a clammy feeling that would overcome him, compelling him to leave the property. He avoided the place except when the bishop came, fearing that his absence would be noticed. The book goes on to report that sometimes an important document will go missing for more than a week, only to turn up exactly where it had been. There was another incident when all the smoke alarms went off at three o'clock in the morning. While searching for the cause with a maintenance worker, a staff member heard very distinct footsteps on the floor above them. They were the only people on the property, and there was no reason for the alarms to go off. One current employee of the center personally told me that he has had experiences on the property but would not elaborate on this further. He only said, "It is a strange place sometimes."

CONCLUSION

Our tour of the Eastern Panhandle's haunts has come to an end. This book is in no way, shape or form a complete collection of the legends and lore of the region. There is easily enough for another complete volume. As I said previously, my purpose with this publication is to highlight some of my favorite tales and the lesser-known ones that have not quite made it into the mainstream pool of folklore. It is my hope that you,

Train station of Harpers Ferry. *Courtesy of the Library of Congress.*

as the reader, appreciate my endeavor to present the most accurate versions of the stories, even if it meant debunking or correcting some previously erroneous information. I have always felt that the truth is scarier than fiction.

Hopefully, you've been entertained and learned something you may not have known about the fascinating history of the area. Are there spirits among us? Or is there, perhaps, an unseen world that is happening around us all the time and only some of us occasionally get glimpses into that world? These are all questions to ponder, and it is up to every one of you to decide for yourselves what the answers are. Whether you believe in ghosts or not, I think we can all agree that the Eastern Panhandle has a rich and fascinating history that has often been unfairly overlooked. I believe history needs to be shared, and if our stories don't continue to be told, they will be forgotten and lost and will not be around for future generations to enjoy.

BIBLIOGRAPHY

The material in this book is drawn from an endless assortment of resources. The Library of Congress has a wonderful repository of digitized newspapers that have proven to be an invaluable resource. Perusing past issues of these old newspapers until I was cross-eyed felt worth it whenever I discovered that one little hidden tidbit that was the missing piece of the puzzle. Issues of the *Martinsburg Evening Journal*, *Martinsburg Statesman*, *Martinsburg Herald*, *Martinsburg Independent* and *Berkeley and Jefferson Intelligencer* were all sources. Issues of *The Shepherdstown Register*, *Spirit of Jefferson* newspapers were also sourced. Articles from the Berkeley County Historical Society were also utilized. Numerous field interviews were conducted, which are too abundant to name. Some material was drawn from published books, which are listed below.

Aler, F. Vernon. *Aler's History of Martinsburg and Berkeley County, West Virginia.* Mail Publishing, 1888.

Barry, Joseph. *The Strange Story of Harpers Ferry: With Legends of the Surrounding Country*. Thompson Brothers, 1903.

Brown, Stephen. *Haunted Houses of Harpers Ferry.* Little Brown House, 1976.

Dougherty, Shirley. *A Ghostly Tour of Harpers Ferry.* EGMID Publishing, 1982.

Gavanda, Walter, and T. Michael Shoemaker. *A Guide to Haunted West Virginia.* Peter's Creek Publishing, 2001.

Kishbucher, Michael. *The Appalachian Legend of the Wizard Clip.* The History Press, 2023.

Snyder, Lambright Harry, III. *John Snyder 1823–1864: A Soldier and His Family.* Self-published, 1999.

About the Author

Justin Stevens hails from several generations of Berkeley County, West Virginia natives. A lifelong fascination with ghost stories and unsolved mysteries led to the creation of the successful and popular Haunted History and Legends Tours of Martinsburg, West Virginia, in 2014. These stories and further field research and meticulous archival digs eventually evolved into the book *Haunted Martinsburg*, published by The History Press. Passionate in his quest to uncover the facts and lost history behind the myths and legends, Justin has become a respected source for local history and loves his role as local "ghostorian." Destination America has consulted with Justin, and his work has been featured on their paranormal programming as well as the *R.I.P. Files* paranormal series. In his "normal" life, Justin works in the medical field and resides in Martinsburg with his husband and their dog, Rhiannon, and three cats, Ligcia, Annabelle Lee and Morella.